D1759834

SWINDON TOWN
On This Day

SWINDON TOWN
On This Day

*History, Facts & Figures
from Every Day of the Year*

ANDREW HAWES

SWINDON TOWN
On This Day

History, Facts & Figures from Every Day of the Year

All statistics, facts and figures are correct as of 1st August 2010

© Andrew Hawes

Andrew Hawes has asserted his rights in accordance with the Copyright, Designs and Patents Act 1988 to be identified as the author of this work.

Published By:
Pitch Publishing (Brighton) Ltd
A2 Yeoman Gate
Yeoman Way
Durrington
BN13 3QZ

Email: info@pitchpublishing.co.uk
Web: www.pitchpublishing.co.uk

First published 2010

A catalogue record for this book is available from the British Library.

ISBN: 978-1-9054119-1-7

Printed and bound in Malta by Gutenburg Press

To Catherine – for being the occasional burst of sanity within the madness – or vice versa. Either way, it's all good.

ACKNOWLEDGEMENTS

I'd like to thank the Pitch Publishing team, notably Dan Tester, for their patience when dealing with some very stretched deadlines and one rather slothful writer.

I also again, have to owe a debt of thanks to two sources of references, firstly Richard Banyard's fantastic history site which is www.swindon-town-fc.co.uk. He's done an amazing job in cataloguing the club and players and deserves every bit of praise there is. Go lose yourself in his site for an afternoon at work – at least.

Peter Matthews' book on John Trollope is not only interesting about the man, but a great historical chronicle of both the good and bad times at the club. John Trollope: Record Breaker is a valuable resource and a great read. Amazon is your friend.

Other than thanking those people for their good work, I should also say that any errors within are thoroughly my own. Feel free to get in touch through andrew@swindontownbooks.co.uk with any feedback you may have. All figures in the book are up to the end of the 2009/10 season.

INTRODUCTION

I don't think I've had as much fun for a long time as I did at Charlton Athletic back in May. Just when it seemed that my recent burst of optimism about the club was being tested by one performance when good things were so close, the unlikely turnaround and ice-cool five good men in the shoot-out. The atmosphere for the home leg was also superb.

It's all good for the soul after a grim decade where you had to question the various owners', shall we say enthusiasm, for the special thing they had under their care. Despite getting older – and hair having long since confined itself to a being a bit part player in my day-to-day life – I still get that same feeling of anticipation whenever the County Ground floodlights home into view. At times, that has been sorely tested, mainly by those off the field, rather than on.

When reading the book – touch wood – it will revive a few memories of long forgotten afternoons spent at the County Ground, Roots Hall, or any of dozens of other grounds up and down the country – more and more of which are now shopping centres or housing estates.

Despite being hopelessly biased, I think the club has a history, albeit good and bad, that sets it apart from many among the 92 League clubs, and beyond. I hope that's reflected in these pages.

Andrew Hawes

SWINDON TOWN
On This Day

JANUARY

TUESDAY 1st JANUARY 1946

Sam Allen dies a day short of his 78th birthday. Allen served the club in different ways for more than half a century. Having initially joined in 1895, he was put in charge of team affairs for the 1902/03 season. Officially, the board selected the starting XI. Allen signed outstanding players like future England international Harold Fleming, Scottish international defender Jock Walker, the club's all-time record scorer Harry Morris – and many more. Morris also turned Swindon into Southern League contenders – they took the title twice just before World War I as well as reaching the last four of the FA Cup – while he was still in charge when the club gained entry into the Football League. Allen stepped down from his role in team affairs in 1933, but remained club secretary, helping re-assemble things when Swindon was shut down during World War II and the ground requisitioned. Allen was in charge of the first team for more than one thousand games.

SATURDAY 1st JANUARY 1994

Glenn Hoddle returned to the County Ground as Chelsea manager having walked out on the Robins following their promotion to the Premier League. Tabloid promises of a hate-filled reception for Hoddle are a little wide of the mark and Chelsea run out comfortable 3-1 winners, with Swindon's consolation goal coming from Andy Mutch. A future Robins' manager, Dennis Wise, is on target for Chelsea in front of a crowd of 16,261.

MONDAY 1st JANUARY 2007

Swindon travelled to the National Hockey Stadium for a key game in League Two against Milton Keynes Dons. In a hard fought fixture, Lee Peacock finishes off a corner just after the half-hour mark, with keeper Phil Smith then producing an excellent penalty save low to his right from Izale McLeod to keep Town in front. The win left Paul Sturrock's side in fourth place, just one point behind the Dons in second. The victory also completed a double over the former Wimbledon, which proves crucial. At the end of the season, Swindon take the final automatic promotion place by one point, with the MK Dons consigned to the play-offs on the final day of the campaign.

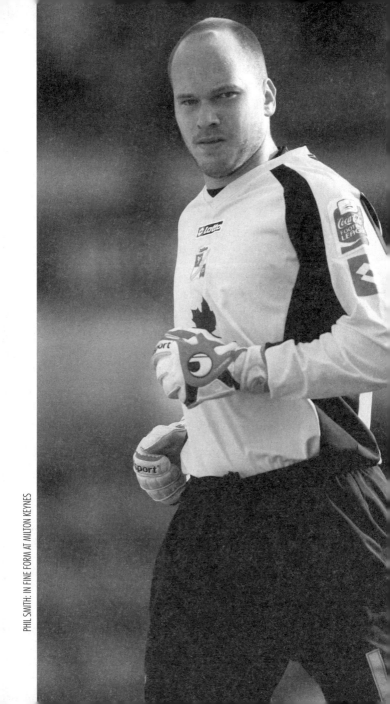

PHIL SMITH: IN FINE FORM AT MILTON KEYNES

SATURDAY 2ND JANUARY 1926

Swindon recover in some style after going 2-0 down at Bournemouth at the County Ground in a Division Three (South) contest. They go on to win 8-2, with forward Frank Richardson, nicknamed 'Swerver', on *Bend It Like Beckham* form. He scored four times, with the other goals coming from Cyril Daniel (2), Jimmy Thompson and Charlie Petrie.

MONDAY 3RD JANUARY 1994

Swindon remain bottom of the Premier League after a televised 1-1 draw with Coventry City at Highfield Road. The audience watching on Sky see Town fall behind to a goal from former Swindon loanee Roy Wegerle, but most don't realise that the game finished 1-1, with the broadcaster suffering technical problems right at the end of the game that caused a blackout. It means that Andy Mutch's equalising volley is only seen by the viewing public via the joys of video tape after the match had finished.

SATURDAY 3RD JANUARY 1998

Steve McMahon's Swindon side, then in the second tier, are shamed by a 2-1 defeat at home to non-league Stevenage Borough in the FA Cup third round. At a rain-lashed and windswept County Ground, Mark Walters uses the conditions to his advantage by scoring with a long-range shot to give Town a fifth-minute lead. Jason Solomon equalised before half-time, and with the vile weather now working in their favour, Giuliano Grazioli scored a second-half winner. As well as the pain of being beaten by Conference opponents, Swindon miss out on a potentially lucrative fourth round match with Premiership side Newcastle United. Eighteen months later, Grazioli would become a Swindon player with Jimmy Quinn bringing him to the County Ground from Peterborough United.

SATURDAY 4TH JANUARY 1986

Lou Macari's Swindon are beaten by Tranmere Rovers in Division Four. Town lost 3-1 at Prenton Park, with Colin Gordon scoring the only Swindon goal via the penalty spot. It proves to be the last defeat of the season as Macari's side go on a 21-game unbeaten run to romp to the league title with 102 points.

SATURDAY 5TH JANUARY 1929

It's just another typical day for Swindon's all-time top scorer Harry Morris. He scored a hat-trick in a 5-0 win over Watford in Division Three (South) at the County Ground. It follows up his three goals the weekend before in a 4-1 local-derby victory against Bristol Rovers at Eastville. Morris ended the season with 31 goals in 43 games – which is actually down on the previous two campaigns.

THURSDAY 5TH JANUARY 1989

Club chairman Brian Hillier, and manager Lou Macari, are charged by the Football Association over bets on Swindon to lose at Newcastle United in their 1988 FA Cup tie. The charges follow allegations by the *Sunday People* newspaper. Town lost the game 5-0 though there were never any claims the match was fixed. It proves to be just the start of the betting and payment issues that would go on to engulf the club and cost Swindon promotion to the old Division One in 1990. The FA hearing on the issue was held more than a year later. It lasted in excess of four hours and saw Brian Hillier banned from football for six months, while Macari was fined £1,000 and warned about his conduct. The club also had to pay a £7,500 fine to the FA. Chief executive Graham Kelly described the results of the hearing as "appropriate penalties".

WEDNESDAY 5TH JANUARY 1972

Swindon's County Ground stages international football as the England under-23 side beat their Welsh counterparts by two goals to nil. Malcolm Macdonald, and man of Wiltshire Mick Channon, score the goals with future Town manager Colin Todd the captain.

SUNDAY 5TH JANUARY 1997

Swindon lose 3-0 at Goodison Park to Everton in an FA Cup third-round tie, mainly thanks to the sending off of Ian Culverhouse after 52 seconds – a cup record. Culverhouse is dismissed for deliberate handball, with Andrei Kanchelskis scoring from the penalty spot. Nick Barmby pounces on a loose back pass to make it two with Duncan Ferguson making it 3-0. Gary Elkins' red card sees Town complete the game with nine men.

TUESDAY 6TH JANUARY 1976

It's a bleak night in the FA Cup as Town lose 2-1 at Tooting & Mitcham in an FA Cup third-round replay, with even the Swindon goal coming via the non-league side's defender Bobby Green. The happiest man is Ron Howell, with the former Robins' midfielder putting one over on his old team. The two sides had drawn 2-2 at the County Ground the previous Saturday.

SATURDAY 7TH JANUARY 1978

There are some kind words from Brian Clough as his Nottingham Forest, the current league champions, beat Swindon 4-1 in the FA Cup at the City Ground in a third-round tie. Dave Moss scored for Town, with Tony Woodcock, Peter Withe and John Robertson netting for Forest in an era where the big names weren't rested for FA Cup ties. Clough was gracious enough to say afterwards: "Swindon played very well and gave us a much harder game than the scoreline suggests. I think we should recognise that."

SATURDAY 8TH JANUARY 1977

Swindon drew 3-3 at Fulham in an entertaining FA Cup tie at Craven Cottage in the era of Fulham's ageing stars. The game proves a Swindon landmark, though, as it sees the final appearance of Don Rogers in a Town shirt in a competitive game as he comes off the bench to replace Colin Prophett. Rogers, constrained by a hip injury, was finding playing more and more difficult, with the great man ultimately needing hip replacement surgery following retirement.

SATURDAY 8TH JANUARY 1983

Swindon enjoyed a merry romp into round four of the FA Cup as they demolished Aldershot 7-0 at the County Ground. Two players score hat-tricks, with Howard Pritchard netting both first-half goals. He grabbed his third in stoppage time. In between that, Andy Rowland scored three times in 16 second-half minutes, with Paul Batty the odd man out. It's the only time since World War II that two Swindon players have scored a hat-trick in the same match. The FA Cup run ended in the next round though, with a 3-1 defeat at Second Division Burnley.

SATURDAY 9TH JANUARY 1926

Swindon beat Clapton 3-2 in an FA Cup third round tie played at West Ham's Upton Park ground. After two goals from 'Swerver' Richardson help Town into a 3-0 lead, Swindon survived a comeback from the Londoners to make it through.

MONDAY 10TH JANUARY 1973

Swindon decide to appoint chief scout Les Allen as manager following the abrupt departure of Dave Mackay and his assistant Des Anderson to Nottingham Forest. Allen had a brief spell in charge of QPR, but this was his first full-time managerial job and it proved to be an unhappy experience. Initially, he was able to help Town secure a further season in the Second Division, finishing in 16th place. The next season, though, money was tight and Allen was sacked with relegation looking inevitable. His reign also saw a falling out with League Cup-winning keeper Peter Downsborough, who was sold to Bradford City. Allen proved to be part of a football dynasty, with his nephew Paul later going on to play for the club.

SATURDAY 11TH JANUARY 1930

Swindon, having a modest season in Division Three (South), headed to Old Trafford to play Division One side Manchester United in the FA Cup third round. They emerged with a superb 2-0 victory. Joe Eddleston put Swindon in front inside the first half hour, with the second via Les Roberts. Goalkeeper Ted Nash produced an outstanding performance to make sure of a memorable Cup upset.

TUESDAY 11TH JANUARY 1977

Fulham bring World Cup winner Bobby Moore, George Best and Rodney Marsh to the County Ground for an FA Cup third-round replay – and they disappear into the Wiltshire night off the back of a 5-0 beating. Dave Syrett (2), Dave Moss (2) and Trevor Anderson score the goals in front of more than 23,000 fans at the County Ground. Town manager Danny Williams highlights the difference between the two teams, saying afterwards: "Fulham have good players, but when they haven't got the ball, they don't work. It's no good having luxury players who don't work hard."

WEDNESDAY 12TH JANUARY 1938

Swindon produce an FA Cup shock to beat First Division, Grimsby Town at the County Ground in a third-round replay, with the game at last bringing some joy for the club's first-ever £1,000 signing, striker Ben Morton. With five minutes left and the Robins trailing 1-0 to a Reg Tomlinson goal, Morton finally scored for the first time in a Swindon shirt – more than two months after arriving from Torquay United. He was buried in the mud afterwards by a heap of ecstatic colleagues. The prolific Alan Fowler scored the winner five minutes from the end of extra time to prevent a second replay and give Swindon a top-flight scalp.

SATURDAY 12TH JANUARY 1963

Swindon's Division Three game with QPR at the County Ground manages to go ahead despite ice and snow across much of the country. Manager Bert Head came up with a master stroke. After minimal warming up, he got the side to wear Bata basketball boots, which help the players' grip no end. The Town players handle the treacherous conditions far better than Rangers and win 5-0, with the visitors making unhappy rumblings. Jack Smith bagged two late goals to score a hat-trick, with the others coming from Don Rogers and Bobby Woodruff. Bata are so delighted their boots prove so effective they use the match as part of a subsequent advertising campaign.

SATURDAY 12TH JANUARY 1991

Swindon record their biggest-ever league win at Ashton Gate, beating neighbours Bristol City 4-0 in a Division Two contest, with Swindon producing some superb passing football under Ossie Ardiles to regularly cut their opponents apart. Town eventually took the lead, after numerous chances, when Micky Hazard's low shot from the edge of the area made it 1-0 at the break. Steve White then produced a glancing header from a Tom Jones cross to make it 2-0 – again after good build-up play. Hazard is then involved once more, breaking free down the left and supplying Duncan Shearer with a close-range header to make it 3-0. White's second came in injury time, completing the scoring by finishing off Jones' cutback. The game ends with City fans turning on their own team.

SATURDAY 13TH JANUARY 1973

Manager Les Allen received a big boost early in his career by guiding Town to a win over top-flight Birmingham City in an FA Cup third-round tie at the County Ground. A second-half goal from Joe Butler, plus a penalty from Irish international Ray Treacy, gave Swindon a 2-0 win. The Birmingham side features the familiar face of League Cup winner Stan Harland at the back, plus a formidable-looking partnership of Trevor Francis and Bob Latchford up front.

SATURDAY 14TH JANUARY 1928

Top scorer Harry Morris finds the net twice to send Swindon through to the FA Cup fourth round with a 2-1 home win over Clapton Orient. It's the last time Swindon won on this day, with ten matches since failing to produce a single victory.

SATURDAY 14TH JANUARY 1978

Ray McHale kept his nerve twice from the spot as his two successful penalties earn Swindon a 2-2 draw with Sheffield Wednesday in a Third Division match at the County Ground. McHale would score 14 penalties during his time with the club before moving to Brighton & Hove Albion.

TUESDAY 15TH JANUARY 2008

After months of negotiation, Swindon's takeover by a consortium led by Andrew Fitton is confirmed. Fitton announces the appointment of former QPR chief executive Nick Watkins, plus backing from Jeremy Wray, Nick Backhouse and businessman Sir Martyn Arbib, a man richer than the Queen. Fitton agrees he will deal with a six-figure tax bill outstanding from the previous regime and also gets a transfer embargo removed. The new board also issue a ten-point plan to try and get the club moving forward. The pledges include long-term plans for the redevelopment of the County Ground, an undertaking to improve communication with supporters, right down to plans to greatly enhance the club shop. Fitton also confirms the appointment of the Scottish international defender Maurice Malpas as manager. It's his first job in English football, with the former Dundee United man seen as something of a left-field choice. Dave Byrne, who has been acting as caretaker boss, is named as his assistant.

THURSDAY 16TH JANUARY 1908

Southern League Swindon record their first-ever win over opponents from the First Division of the Football League – and they do so away from home by beating Sheffield United in the first round of the FA Cup at Bramall Lane. Town win 3-2 after extra time with Jimmy Johnston, Frank Warburton and Billy Tout the scorers.

FRIDAY 16TH JANUARY 1998

Steve McMahon pays £30,000 to Nottingham Forest for midfielder Bobby Howe, who has experience of Uefa Cup football. He makes his debut the next day against Reading. Howe never really became popular with fans and struggled to make an impression in the years when the club was struggling, before he was released in 2002. However, he did briefly inspire a chant of "Bobby Howe's sexy football" during an away game at Port Vale.

SATURDAY 17TH JANUARY 1970

Swindon earned their first-ever victory over Leicester City, a 2-0 win at Filbert Street in the Second Division. Striker Arthur Horsfield scored twice past Peter Shilton as Town keep up the pressure on the sides at the top of the table. Horsfield's double saw the striker continue to find the score-sheet regularly after costing a club record £17,500 from Newcastle United the previous summer. He would go on to score 28 goals in his first season, six of those in the Anglo-Italian Cup.

THURSDAY 17TH JANUARY 1963

Future Swindon striker Colin Gordon is born on this day. Gordon was plucked from non-league obscurity with Oldbury United by manager Lou Macari in 1984. Macari proved to have a good eye for talent, whenever it can be found, and he soon settled into life in the Football League, finding the score-sheet regularly. Gordon went on to be top scorer in the 1984/85 season, scoring 17 times in 35 games. He then netted 16 times in the 1985/86 championship campaign. The front man's form earned him a £100,000 move to Wimbledon. After a nomadic playing career, Gordon went on to become a successful football agent, forming Key Sports Management, representing Steve McClaren and attacking corruption within the sport.

TUESDAY 18TH JANUARY 1994

Striker Jan Age Fjortoft scored his first Swindon goal as Town went out of the FA Cup in a third-round replay with Ipswich at Portman Road. Fjortoft looked to be heading back to Norway on loan after failing to score during a disastrous first half of the season following his £500,000 move from Rapid Vienna. After scoring, Fjortoft sank to his haunches and clenched both fists in a celebration of pure relief. The rest is history; a transformed Fjortoft scoring goals that proved to be some of the highlights of the club's only Premier League campaign.

SATURDAY 18TH JANUARY 2003

Swindon travelled to Stockport County in a Division Two game and won 5-2, with five different players getting on the score-sheet. Sam Parkin and Steve Robinson got Town going with goals inside the first 15 minutes, with second-half strikes from Alan Reeves, Matt Hewlett and finally Eric Sabin.

THURSDAY 19TH JANUARY 2006

Manager Iffy Onuora made a double signing as Swindon battled to avoid relegation back into the bottom tier of the Football League. He brought in striker Lee Peacock on a permanent deal from Sheffield Wednesday and winger Albert Jarrett on loan from Brighton & Hove Albion. Both players came off the bench to help secure a 4-2 win over AFC Bournemouth at the County Ground. While Jarrett would suffer a car crash and play just six games during his stay, Peacock would prove to be a popular and valuable player, most notably in the 2006/07 promotion season back into League One, becoming a useful central midfielder. After 21 goals and more than 100 games, Peacock eventually moved to Grimsby Town in January 2010, with a combination of injuries and on-pitch success forcing him to seek first-team football elsewhere.

THURSDAY 20TH JANUARY 1994

Swindon boss John Gorman turned to Brian Kilcline to try and organise his Premier League defence, paying Newcastle United £90,000 for the 31-year-old FA Cup winner. He helps Town to a 2-1 win over Spurs on his debut and inspires a brief spell where ponytail baseball caps go on sale in the club shop. He ends up playing just 24 matches.

SATURDAY 21st JANUARY 1961

Bert Head's Swindon side scored a comfortable 4-0 win over Bury in Division Three, with two goals each at the County Ground for Cliff Jackson and Mike Summerbee. The side included just two players who weren't brought up through the Swindon system or picked up from local non-league sides as youngsters. They are Arnold Darcy and Fred Jones. The side in full: Burton, Wollen, Trollope, Morgan, Owen, Woodruff, Darcy, Hunt, Summerbee, Jackson and Jones.

TUESDAY 22nd JANUARY 1980

Swindon's remarkable League Cup run continues with a 2-1 semi-final first-leg win over First Division Wolves to give Bobby Smith's side a genuine chance of a trip to Wembley. Prolific strike force Andy Rowland and Alan Mayes both score. Rowland heads home Chris Kamara's cross and Mayes grabs the winner with four minutes to go following Peter Daniel's equaliser. It earns Swindon a one-goal lead to take back to Molineux for the second leg. Manager Bobby Smith felt his side could have played better.

SATURDAY 22nd JANUARY 1983

Teenage striker Paul Rideout underlined his potential by scoring the second hat-trick of his career. Rideout was just 18 at the time and his goals helped Swindon ease past Rochdale 4-1 in a Division Four fixture at the County Ground. Rideout completed his hat-trick after 54 minutes, with a late strike from Howard Pritchard adding to the scoring. Rideout would score 20 league goals in the 1982/83 season and the club were unable to resist a £250,000 offer for him from Aston Villa once the campaign ended.

TUESDAY 22nd JANUARY 2008

Maurice Malpas' Town side suffer a penalty shoot-out exit in an FA Cup third-round replay at Barnet. The game finished 1-1 after extra time, with Billy Paynter scoring at both ends. Swindon were unable to take advantage of playing the additional 30 minutes with a man advantage after Michael Leary's red card. Then came the horror of spot-kicks as all four Town players missed to make unwanted FA Cup history. Billy Paynter, Christan Roberts, Hasney Aljofree and Miguel Comminges all contrived to miss in different ways as Barnet go through 2-0. The Underhill slope is no excuse.

SATURDAY 23RD JANUARY 1965

It's the meeting of the two most loyal men in football at the County Ground as Swindon play Portsmouth in a Division Three fixture, with John Trollope and Jimmy Dickinson lining up opposite each other. Left-half Dickinson, an England international in his prime, was en route to making 764 league appearances for Portsmouth. That was to be the record for one club until Trollope topped it, playing 770 league games for Town. The game finished 0-0.

FRIDAY 24TH JANUARY 1986

After much wrangling, Swindon goalkeeper Scott Endersby finally completed the move he wanted from the County Ground, with Carlisle United paying £5,000 for his signature after a loan spell. After being voted Player of the Season for 1984/85, Enderbsy was dropped early in the 1985/86 campaign in favour of Kenny Allen. Endersby returned with Allen cup-tied in October as Swindon scored an upset win over Sunderland in the League Cup. At this point the argument came to a head, with Endersby wanting to play or be released as Allen returned for the next league game. The club say Endersby demanded a free transfer, while he insisted it was more complicated. Either way the Sunderland match was the last of his 100 Town appearances.

SATURDAY 24TH JANUARY 1988

Swindon grabbed an injury-time draw with Bradford City in Division One after an entertaining game at Valley Parade. Chris Hay's volley made it 1-1 in stoppage time in front of a crowd of 15,130.

WEDNESDAY 25TH JANUARY 2006

Swindon, struggling to avoid relegation into League Two, made the decision to sell top scorer Rory Fallon to Swansea City for £300,000. His contract was due to run out in the summer. A bruising striker signed from Barnsley, Fallon had really come into his own after the departure of the prolific Sam Parkin. He scored 14 goals in 28 games in the 2005/06 campaign. Following his departure, Swindon scored just 17 more times in the remaining 18 matches in League One as they suffered relegation. The Kiwi ended the season as the club's top scorer despite his premature exit.

SATURDAY 25TH JANUARY 2003

Swindon recorded an impressive win over Wigan Athletic in Division Two at the County Ground. The Latics suffered just four defeats all season but Town won 2-1 with first-half goals from Danny Invincible and Andy Gurney.

TUESDAY 25TH JANUARY 2005

Town suffered a 2-0 defeat at Southend United in the Southern Area semi-finals of the LDV Vans Trophy, with Swindon having never gone any further than this stage of the competition under its many sponsors. Nicky Nicolau, a flop at the County Ground, is one of the Southend scorers.

SATURDAY 26TH JANUARY 1980

Swindon held Tottenham Hotspur to a more than creditable 0-0 draw in an FA Cup fourth-round tie at the County Ground in front of 26,000 fans, with future managers Ossie Ardiles and Glenn Hoddle in the Spurs line-up. The performance is all the more impressive coming just four days after the League Cup semi-final first leg with Wolverhampton Wanderers.

MONDAY 26TH JANUARY 2009

Swindon manager Danny Wilson signs four players as he looks to rebuild the squad he inherited from Maurice Malpas and prevent a return to League Two. Wilson brings in centre-half Gordon Greer, on loan from Doncaster Rovers, and Reading winger Hal Robson-Kanu. There are also two arrivals from French football, Haitian defender Lescinel Jean-Francois and a forward picked up from the amateur leagues, Hamdi Razak. Greer and Robson-Kanu both make their debuts the following night, helping Town to a nervy 3-2 win against Walsall which is the start of a useful five-match unbeaten run.

TUESDAY 26TH JANUARY 2010

Swindon scored an emphatic 3-0 win over Leeds United at the County Ground with both sides looking for promotion from League One. Charlie Austin gets things going with a low drive after being set up by Simon Ferry in the first half. Billy Paynter headed in Lescinel Jean-Francois' cross to make it 2-0, before stroking home a penalty shortly afterwards. The win moved Town into fifth place, ten points behind Leeds in second.

SATURDAY 27TH JANUARY 1968

Swindon, then in the Third Division, scored a modest FA Cup exit by beating Second Division Blackburn Rovers in a third-round game at the County Ground, with cultured centre-back Mel Nurse scoring the only goal of the game. It's a fine response to a defeat by Northampton Town the previous Saturday.

SATURDAY 27TH JANUARY 1973

It's now seven league games without a win for Swindon in Division Two as Les Allen's side lose 2-0 at Blackpool's Bloomfield Road. Alan Suddick and Billy Rafferty's goals go unanswered on the Lancashire coast.

WEDNESDAY 27TH JANUARY 1982

Future Swindon goalkeeper Rhys Evans is born in the town. Evans joined the club in the summer of 2003 having been released by Chelsea, opting to sign for his home town club despite apparent interest from clubs higher up the pyramid. The England under-21 keeper went on to spend three seasons with Town, rejecting overtures from Leeds United at one stage. Evans helped the side reach the play-offs in his first campaign and he was named Player of the Year in the 2005/06 relegation season before leaving the club to sign for Blackpool.

TUESDAY 28TH JANUARY 1969

Having booked their place in the League Cup Final in December, Swindon showed their focus was very much on securing promotion to Division Two as they thumped Oldham Athletic 5-1 in a Division Three game at the County Ground. Swindon were 2-0 up after four minutes with striker Chris Jones going on to complete a hat-trick. Frank Burrows and Roger Smart also scored, with a highly impressive crowd of 21,316 in attendance.

FRIDAY 28TH JANUARY 1994

With Fraser Digby ruled out via a dislocated shoulder picked up at Hillsborough and other worries, Swindon signed Cambridge United's back-up keeper Jon Sheffield on a month's loan. Sheffield made his debut in a 5-0 defeat by Aston Villa at Villa Park, and then went off injured in his second and final game, a thrilling 3-3 draw with Norwich City.

WEDNESDAY 29th JANUARY 1930

Swindon suffered their worst cup defeat ever, losing 10-1 to First Division Manchester City at Maine Road. Bobby Marshall scored five past back-up keeper Herbie Webster, who was unable to follow up Ted Nash's fine performance in the third-round win at Manchester United. Harry Morris scored Town's only goal. Swindon returned to Manchester City 23 years later in the same competition and things improved, but only marginally – it's 7-0 this time.

SATURDAY 29th JANUARY 1966

Swindon made the short trip to promoted neighbours Oxford United for a first-ever competitive visit to the Manor Ground. Town ran out comfortable 3-0 winners in the Division Three contest. Scottish outside-right Tom Henderson opened the scoring early, with Dennis Brown making it 2-0 before the break. Mel Nurse then completed victory with a late goal on 88 minutes.

SATURDAY 29th JANUARY 1977

Swindon and Everton played out a cracking 2-2 FA Cup fourth-round draw at the County Ground on what, by modern standards, looked like a glorified beach. Town twice fell behind – firstly to Duncan McKenzie's finish from a high ball into the area. The Swindon response came from a partially blocked Ray McHale shot from a free kick that Dave Syrett pounced on and tucked past David Lawson. The second half saw Everton reclaim the lead from a cleverly worked short-corner routine that was finished off by Bob Latchford. Then came the defining moment of the match… Kenny Stroud ignored the bobbly surface to let rip a 30-yard first-time shot that crashed into the top corner in front of the Town End. It's such a good strike it makes the HTV Goal of the Season shortlist. Swindon ride out the last half hour of the game to earn a replay at Goodison Park.

SUNDAY 30th JANUARY 1944

Future Swindon defender Frank Burrows was born in Larkhall, Scotland. Burrows turned out to be an astute signing by Danny Williams, joining from Scunthorpe United in the summer of 1968. He was a key part of the 1969 League Cup and promotion-winning side and played more than 300 games before a successful coaching career.

SATURDAY 30th JANUARY 1988

A Swindon side with back-up keeper Nicky Hammond in goal were handsomely beaten in the FA Cup by First Division Newcastle United, losing 5-0 at St. James' Park. Paul Gascoigne was in particularly fine form, scoring twice. While the result in itself was frustrating, the repercussions from the game would haunt the club over the next two-and-a-half years. It would begin with a newspaper story showing chairman Brian Hillier and manager Lou Macari had had a bet on the club to lose. This resulted in a suspension for Hillier and a fine for the club and Macari. Subsequent newspaper articles would then make allegations of illegal payments to players which would be punished by the Football League with an almost immediate demotion from the top flight in 1990 after the play-off final win at Wembley. As well as the hurt of missing out on Division One football for the first time, the club was left with a tarnished image despite a spectacular rise up the leagues under Macari and Ossie Ardiles.

FRIDAY 31st JANUARY 1997

Swindon sold midfielder Kevin Horlock to Division One rivals Manchester City for a then club record figure of £1.5m. After being signed by Glenn Hoddle as cover at left-back for Paul Bodin, Horlock went on to become a highly effective and free-scoring midfielder under Steve McMahon, netting 16 times in the Division Two championship season of 1995/96 and continuing to be a danger to defences back in Division One. His move left him stuck on 199 Swindon appearances.

TUESDAY 31st JANUARY 1967

Three World Cup winners were sent home from Wiltshire humbled as Swindon beat West Ham United 3-1 in their FA Cup third-round replay. The Hammers side which included Martin Peters, Bobby Moore and Geoff Hurst were, at times, unable to deal with Swindon's attacking play. Willie Penman gave Swindon a first-half lead, but John Sissons kept the Hammers in it by scoring with 12 minutes to go. Town kept pushing, and John Trollope's break forward from full-back set up Don Rogers to score, with Ken Skeen wrapping things up late on. Around 2,000 fans missed the match as they were locked out, with the official attendance 25,789.

SWINDON TOWN
On This Day

FEBRUARY

TUESDAY 1st FEBRUARY 1977

Swindon suffered a cruel defeat in the FA Cup at Goodison Park in a fourth-round replay against an Everton side featuring Bruce Rioch and future manager Andy King. Trevor Anderson put Third Division Swindon in front with just 11 minutes to go. Martin Dobson conjured up an equaliser just two minutes later before Dave Jones' injury-time winner ended hopes of a major upset.

SATURDAY 1st FEBRUARY 1997

Defender Gary Elkins scored his only Swindon goal as Town see off Sheffield United 2-1 in a Division One game at the County Ground. Elkins, £80,000 worth of left-back signed from Wimbledon, would only play 26 games for the club before being released and drifting into non-league football.

SATURDAY 2nd FEBRUARY 1985

Swindon record a 1-0 win over Mansfield Town at the County Ground in Division Four under player-manager Lou Macari. A crowd of 2,664 is sent home happy thanks to a late Peter Coyne goal. The game clearly created a lasting impression on Macari though, as the Stags' defence featured a defender called Colin Calderwood. Macari went on to sign him that summer via a tribunal, with the fee a modest £27,500. The Scotsman was immediately made club captain and goes on to be one of the greatest centre-backs in Swindon history.

SUNDAY 3rd FEBRUARY 1974

The County Ground staged Sunday football for the first time in a 2-2 draw with Bolton Wanderers in Division Two, with Ray Clarke and Terry Hubbard scoring for the Robins. A crowd of 8,835 came through the turnstiles – more than double the attendance for the previous game at home to Hull City. The build-up to the game is dominated by Scottish goalkeeper Jimmy Allan. Allan, who was brought up as part of a strict Scottish Presbyterian church, said he couldn't play on the Sabbath day as it went against his beliefs. Manager Les Allen agreed and Alan Spratley took over in goal. The Scot is restored back into the starting line-up for the next game, a 3-0 defeat at Millwall.

SUNDAY 4TH FEBRUARY 1990

Swindon record a memorable 3-2 win over the league leaders Leeds United in the race for promotion from Division Two – it's Swindon's first-ever win over the Yorkshire side. Gordon Strachan slotted home a penalty to put Leeds in front before Steve White set up Alan McLoughlin with an unselfish header. Steve Foley nodded in David Kerslake's cross to make it 2-1 before John Hendrie pulled a goal back. Ross McLaren's low drive smacks off the post just three minutes later to give Swindon the win with a performance manager Ossie Ardiles describes as their best of the season. The victory leaves Ardiles' side six points behind Sheffield United in second place.

SATURDAY 5TH FEBRUARY 1994

Striker Jan Age Fjortoft scored his first Swindon hat-trick as Town easily saw off Coventry City to record a 3-1 Premiership win. Fjortoft netted with two first-half penalties and wrapped up the game with his third with 11 minutes to go after Julian Darby pulled a goal back for Coventry. The game saw the birth of Fjortoft's trademark aeroplane celebration and was the beginning of a run of 11 goals in 15 games that would transform the Norwegian from apparent flop to cult hero.

TUESDAY 5TH FEBRUARY 1985

Swindon were beaten in their first-ever competitive penalty shoot-out, losing 4-3 on spot kicks to Torquay United in the Freight Rover Trophy after the tie finished level 1-1 on aggregate. After the Gulls showed some early nerves by failing to score with two of their first three attempts, two misses from Paul Batty and Andy Rowland meant that Town were back up against it, with future Swindon goalkeeper Kenny Allen producing two saves to deny them. The shoot-out goes to sudden death, with Torquay's Steve Pugh making it 4-3, only for Allen to produce his third stop by blocking Colin Bailie's spot kick.

FRIDAY 5TH FEBRUARY 1960

Future Swindon midfielder Micky Hazard was born in Sunderland. Signed by his old Spurs colleague Ossie Ardiles, Hazard played more than 140 games over four seasons, becoming an integral part of a ball-playing Swindon midfield before heading back to White Hart Lane.

FRIDAY 6TH FEBRUARY 1987

Swindon complete the loan signing of left-back Phil King from Torquay United in time for him to make his debut the following day against Blackpool. A little over a month later, he was signed on a permanent basis for £17,500. He quickly went on to fill the left-back position, helping Town to promotion in the play-offs against Gillingham at the end of the season, and carrying on as a first-team regular until he was sold to Sheffield Wednesday in 1990 for a then club record £400,000. A brief return followed in 1997 under Steve McMahon, though that lasted just five matches before the two reportedly fell out. Nowadays, Phil can be heard as an astute summariser as part of BBC Radio Wiltshire's Swindon Town radio commentaries.

SATURDAY 6TH FEBRUARY 1993

Paul Bodin's low drive was enough to give Swindon a 1-0 win at Sunderland's Roker Park as they chased promotion to the Premier League. Bodin's goal arrived early in the second half. It's the third 1-0 victory in a row for Glenn Hoddle's side, with the Welsh left-back getting the goal on each occasion. Bodin would go on to score 12 goals that season in total, most notably the penalty that would earn Town a place in the top flight by beating Leicester City at Wembley.

SATURDAY 7TH FEBRUARY 2004

Northamptonshire side Rushden & Diamonds made their first-ever visit to the County Ground in a Division Two fixture, with Swindon looking to maintain their challenge for the play-offs. Town went 2-0 up in the first 20 minutes with goals from Tommy Mooney and Andy Gurney's penalty. When Alan Reeves, not under pressure, sliced a cross into his own net it gave the Diamonds some hope. David Duke's neat shot restored the two-goal cushion, only for Rodney Jack to make it 3-2 a minute later. Town finally killed off their opponents in injury time, when Diamonds defender Barry Hunter put through his own net under pressure from Rory Fallon. The victory leaves Swindon in fourth place, but nine points behind the second side QPR with a third of the season to go. Rushden were ultimately relegated.

WEDNESDAY 8TH FEBRUARY 1984

Swindon cruised past Chester City in a Division Four game at Sealand Road, courtesy of two first-half strikes from Garry Nelson and a third from Paul Batty. All three goals arrived in the opening 45 minutes of play. The attendance is a mostly nonplussed 880, with the Blues on course to finished bottom of the Football League and Town recording their lowest-ever league placing at the end of the season, 17th in Division Four – under manager Ken Beamish. The 880 figure is the lowest post-war attendance for a Swindon first-team game.

THURSDAY 8TH FEBRUARY 1979

Swindon boss Bobby Smith paid out £80,000 to land Watford striker Alan Mayes. It proved to be money well spent, with Mayes and Andy Rowland going on to strike up one of the club's happiest striker partnerships. Mayes began life failing to dislodge the likes of Stan Bowles at QPR before arriving in Wiltshire after a successful period at Vicarage Road. Mayes scored 39 goals in 89 league starts in his first spell with Swindon, and also played a key role in the 1979/80 League Cup semi-final run with goals against Arsenal in the quarter-final, and Wolverhampton Wanderers in the first leg of the semi-final. His impressive record tempted Chelsea, then in Division Two, to pay £200,000 to lure him away in December 1980. Two and a half years later, Mayes returned to the County Ground on a free transfer and still managed to find the net 20 times in the bleak 1983/84 season, before leaving the club in the summer of 1985. Mayes, a reliable penalty taker, scored 83 goals in a Swindon shirt, putting him in a tie for 12th in the club's all-time scoring list.

SATURDAY 8TH FEBRUARY 1992

Captain Colin Calderwood starred in a 2-1 defeat of Brighton & Hove Albion at the County Ground. With Town falling behind early in the first half, the centre-half turned things around with two goals in 11 minutes to help Glenn Hoddle's side to three welcome points. It was the first time Calderwood had scored a brace in his Town career, almost seven years after he was signed by Lou Macari.

SATURDAY 9TH FEBRUARY 1957

Swindon's poor season in Division Three (South) reached a nadir with a second 7-0 defeat of the season. After losing to Bournemouth & Boscombe in September, Town were thumped by the same score at Torquay United at Plainmoor, with Sammy Collins netting a hat-trick. It proved a tough first season in charge for manager Bert Head. After finishing 23rd, Swindon were forced to apply for re-election at the end of the campaign.

SATURDAY 9TH FEBRUARY 1980

Manager Bobby Smith picked his strongest side just three days before the second leg of the League Cup semi-final. But, perhaps understandably, Swindon lost 2-1 at home to Sheffield Wednesday in a Division Three game at the County Ground. Both sides had realistic promotion aspirations, but the visitors came away with the win after a late strike from Kevin Taylor. Swindon's goal is a penalty from Ray McHale.

SATURDAY 10TH FEBRUARY 1912

Swindon forward Harold Fleming starred for England in an international match against Ireland. Fleming scored a hat-trick in England's 6-1 victory in Dublin. The game was the first match in the British Home Championship, which England and Scotland went on to share. In Fleming's absence, Town were beaten 2-0 at Reading in the Southern League.

TUESDAY 10TH FEBRUARY 1976

Five different players scored for Swindon as they beat Aldershot 6-3 in a Division Three contest at the County Ground. Ulsterman Trevor Anderson netted two penalties, with the other goals coming from Dave Syrett, Will Dixon, Kenny Stroud and David Moss. Future Swindon assistant manager Malcolm Crosby came off the bench as a substitute for the Shots. It made it five games unbeaten for Danny Williams' side who were in the relegation zone in January.

SATURDAY 10TH FEBRUARY 1996

Swindon kept on course for immediate promotion out of Division Two by beating Swansea City 1-0 at the Vetch Field with a Shaun Taylor goal. It proved to be the only game in charge for Swans boss Kevin Cullis, surreally appointed from non-league Cradley Heath.

SATURDAY 11TH FEBRUARY 1967

Swindon lost 1-0 at Doncaster Rovers in Division Three, with Town unable to conjure up a reply to Tony Coleman's goal at the start of the second half. It would become a familiar story – no Town side has ever come away from Belle Vue, or Rovers' Keepmoat Stadium, with a victory. Rovers went on to be relegated, with Swindon finishing in eighth place.

TUESDAY 12TH FEBRUARY 1980

Swindon were controversially beaten 3-1 by Wolverhampton Wanderers in the second leg of their League Cup semi-final. The Midlands side went through 4-3 on aggregate to earn a trip to Wembley, with the game exploding to life in the second half. Two goals in six second-half minutes put Wolves in front for the first time, with Town having a Billy Tucker effort disallowed. The defining moment came when keeper Paul Bradshaw sprinted out to attempt to deal with a long ball into the penalty area. Alan Mayes got there first, beyond defender George Berry. As he attempted to bring the ball under control and get his shot away, Bradshaw clattered into him in a brutal collision, which left Mayes needing stitches. He always looked second best to get the ball. Referee Neil Midgley awarded the penalty, but no more – these days Bradshaw would almost certainly have been given a red card for denying a clear goalscoring opportunity. Ray McHale tucked away the spot kick, and the tie was level on aggregate. But Wolves scored once more through Mel Eves, to move ahead 4-3 on aggregate and close out the game to leave Swindon one step short of a return to Wembley.

SUNDAY 12TH FEBRUARY 1995

Swindon beat Bolton Wanderers 2-1 in the first leg of the League Cup semi-finals at the County Ground, with Peter Thorne scoring twice. After falling behind to an early goal from Alan Stubbs, Town levelled things up when Thorne was there to turn home Jan Age Fjortoft's blocked shot. Thorne then scored the key second with 14 minutes to go. The late sending off of defender Mark Robinson was not enough to prevent Steve McMahon's side taking a narrow lead to Burnden Park for the second leg, which was to be held almost a month later.

TUESDAY 12TH FEBRUARY 2008

Swindon finally beat neighbours Cheltenham Town for the first time since the Gloucestershire side won promotion into the Football League. Goals from Simon Cox, Billy Paynter and Christian Roberts gave one set of Robins a comfortable 3-0 win in the League One contest at the County Ground. The record against Cheltenham remains poor though, with that victory the only success in eight meetings between the two sides.

TUESDAY 13TH FEBRUARY 1962

Swindon midfielder Charlie Henry was born on this day. Having come through the club's youth system Henry initially broke into the first team as a full-back, playing regularly as Town slipped into Division Four for the first time. Henry's career was revitalised, like the club, by Lou Macari. He decided to convert the defender into an attacking midfielder, with spectacular results. Henry plundered 18 league goals to be the club's top scorer in the 1985/86 Division Four championship season, twice netting hat-tricks. With the move up a division, Henry faded from view and was loaned out to Torquay United and Northampton Town. However, he arrived as cavalry in the Division Three play-offs. Henry came on as a half-time substitute in the home leg with Gillingham, with Swindon needing to score twice. After Peter Coyne pulled one back, Henry's thunderous volley squared the tie on aggregate, forcing a third game. He eventually left the club at the end of the 1988/89 season, after making 269 appearances.

TUESDAY 13TH FEBRUARY 2001

Swindon manager Andy King paid £50,000 to Birmingham City for midfielder Steve Robinson, who would get the nickname 'Turbo'. He quickly won over fans through his energetic displays – and two volleys at Oxford United in a 2-0 win at the Manor Ground that helped Swindon edge to Division Two survival. A broken leg at Blackpool in January 2004 saw Robinson go through a tough season and a half – at one point he was allowed to go and train with other clubs – but he battled his way back into favour and got an excellent reception in his final game in May 2005 against Chesterfield when he came on as a second-half substitute. Robinson racked up 158 games in his four-and-a-half seasons in Wiltshire.

SATURDAY 14TH FEBRUARY 1981

Andy Rowland brings joy to Swindon hearts on Valentine's Day with a hat-trick as Swindon score an emphatic 5-2 victory over Sheffield United in Division Three. Rowland's three goals, plus an Ian Miller effort and a penalty from Brian Williams, meant Swindon were 5-0 up at one stage. It's the biggest win of the 1980/81 season and proved crucial in the final analysis. Swindon stayed up by just one point in 17th place, while the Blades finished 21st and made the drop into Division Four.

THURSDAY 14TH FEBRUARY 2002

Swindon and Reading play out a 0-0 draw in Division Two in a match that saw three red cards handed out by referee Barry Knight. The Royals' Sammy Igoe is dismissed late in the first half for two bookable offences, but Town were unable to take advantage. Late on, substitute Paul McAreavey lasted just four minutes before being given a straight red for a challenge on John Mackie. Then in stoppage time, it became nine versus ten as Alan Reeves was also dismissed for kicking out.

SATURDAY 15TH FEBRUARY 1935

Swindon end a dismal run of five defeats, shipping 20 goals in the process, as they beat Millwall 3-1 at the County Ground in Division Three (South). Manager Ted Vizard saw Frank Peters (2) and Alan Fowler score in front of a crowd of just 4,645.

SATURDAY 15TH FEBRUARY 1969

Swindon made what proves to be their final Football League visit to Holker Street (for now) for a Division Three game with Barrow. Danny Williams' side won 3-0 on their way to promotion, with a goal each for Roger Smart, Peter Noble and Chris Jones.

TUESDAY 15TH FEBRUARY 1994

Winger Alex Henshall is born on this day. Henshall is considered a bright enough prospect to be named on the bench at the age of 15 for a Johnstone's Paint Trophy tie at Exeter City, and was soon snapped up by Manchester City before playing a first-team game.

SATURDAY 16TH FEBRUARY 1929

Swindon hold First Division Arsenal to a 0-0 draw in the FA Cup fifth round at the County Ground. Arsenal manager Herbert Chapman, who had a brief spell at Swindon as a player, employs an extra defender to contain prolific striker Harry Morris. Swindon push hard in the replay the following Wednesday, only losing 1-0.

SUNDAY 16TH FEBRUARY 1992

The *Match of the Day* cameras headed to the County Ground for an FA Cup fifth-round clash between Swindon and Premier League side Aston Villa. With Swindon going for the play-offs, the TV companies hoped for an upset. They got a game featuring some neat football, but a win for Aston Villa, who went 2-0 up through Dwight Yorke and Steve Froggatt. Dave Mitchell's goal 14 minutes from time proved not to be enough for Swindon, with the game finishing 2-1.

SATURDAY 17TH FEBRUARY 1973

Swindon found QPR in irresistible form in a Division Two meeting at Loftus Road. Stan Bowles focused on football rather than horses to bag a hat-trick as Rangers won 5-0, with the other goals coming from Gerry Francis and Don Givens. A strong-looking Rangers line-up also included Phil Parkes in goal, Terry Venables and Terry Mancini.

SATURDAY 17TH FEBRUARY 1996

Swindon continued their FA Cup run with a 1-1 draw against Premier League Southampton in the fifth round. Kevin Horlock delighted the County Ground as Town opened the scoring, beating keeper Dave Beasant with a low shot after a delightful team passing move. Gordon Watson, one of Swindon's Premiership nemeses, headed home an equaliser from a vicious Matt Le Tissier corner to take the two sides back to The Dell.

WEDNESDAY 18TH FEBRUARY 1987

Swindon goalkeeper Fraser Digby made his England under-21 debut in a friendly against Spain in Burgos. Digby came off the bench as England won 2-1. Digby went on to gain a further four caps for England at under-21 level.

SAINTS: KEVIN HORLOCK'S BURIED AFTER SCORING VERSUS THE SAINTS

SUNDAY 18TH FEBRUARY 1990

Swindon fans expecting to welcome Lou Macari back to the County Ground as West Ham United boss find him absent from their Division Two fixture. Macari had resigned after the Hammers board failed to support him in his appeal against his fine over betting on Swindon to lose in their FA Cup defeat at Newcastle United. On the pitch, the sides battled to a 2-2 draw. Steve White and Ross MacLaren's goals were sandwiched in between two efforts from former Swindon striker Jimmy Quinn.

SATURDAY 19TH FEBRUARY 1949

Trusty striker Maurice Owen came good as Swindon enjoyed a derby-day victory over Bristol City at Ashton Gate in Division Three (South). Owen scored twice with Jimmy Bain netting once in a 3-1 victory.

SATURDAY 19TH FEBRUARY 1994

Swindon came within seven minutes of getting off the foot of the Premier League table as they played out an enthralling 3-3 draw with Norwich City at the County Ground. Swindon came from 1-0 down to go 3-2 up at one stage, with two goals from the reborn Jan Age Fjortoft, while keeper Jon Sheffield was forced off with an injury to be replaced by Nicky Hammond. Jeremy Goss made it 3-3 late on though as Town's defensive frailties continued to be exposed in the top flight.

SATURDAY 20TH FEBRUARY 1999

Swindon let victory slip away as they draw 3-3 with Portsmouth in a remarkable Division One meeting at the County Ground. Swindon swept into the lead with two goals from Chris Hay and looked in an unassailable position with Pompey keeper Aaron Flahavan going off with a broken cheekbone after a clash with Iffy Onuora as the two contested a high ball. With no substitute keeper on the bench, Portsmouth were forced to put defender Russell Perrett in goal. By half-time it was 3-1. Despite the handicap, Portsmouth rip back into Swindon – Steve Claridge scored again, then Jeff Peron completed the visiting side's comeback.

SATURDAY 21st FEBRUARY 1971

Swindon's best post-war FA Cup run is brought to an end by Leeds United in the last eight of the competition. Leeds eased through to the semi-finals, earning a 2-0 win on a muddy County Ground pitch. Alan Clarke scored both Leeds goals – he took advantage of Stan Harland missing a header to round Peter Downsborough for the first, while a clinical finish following Mick Jones' approach play effectively killed off the tie before half-time.

SATURDAY 21st FEBRUARY 2009

Swindon came back from 2-0 down to record a 4-2 home win against a Scunthorpe United side who were reduced to nine men in a League One fixture. Danny Wilson's side trailed 2-0 at the break after goals from Gary Hooper and Henri Lansbury. The match gradually began to turn when Iron defender Cliff Byrne was sent off for two yellow cards. Scunthorpe were then down to nine as David Mirfin earned a second booking for tripping Simon Cox. It left Town half an hour to rescue something. Michael Timlin netted from the edge of the area soon after to make it 2-1, then with 19 minutes left, Andrew Wright sliced an Anthony McNamee cross into his own net. After ferocious pressure, loanee Hal Robson-Kanu made it 3-2 with eight minutes left, before Lee Peacock forced home the fourth with five minutes to spare.

SATURDAY 22nd FEBRUARY 1936

Swindon have local bragging rights with Reading after a 4-1 home victory in Division Three (South). Outside-left Tom Wells scored a hat-trick in his only season at the County Ground, with Alan Fowler chipping in with the other goal.

WEDNESDAY 23rd FEBRUARY 2005

Swindon beat Port Vale 1-0 in League One in front of just 4,724 fans but it was a rewarding experience for some of those who did make it. Michael Proctor, signed on loan from Rotherham United, scored the only goal of the game. Proctor's wages had been partly paid for by the Red Army Fund – money raised by a group of fans specifically to allow the manager some extra flexibility when it came to bringing in new players, rather than an investment in the club that might disappear into the darker mysteries of boardroom affairs.

SATURDAY 24TH FEBRUARY 1979

Striker Alan Mayes made a spectacular impact on his debut after his move from Watford earlier in the month. The £80,000 signing scored a 20-minute hat-trick either side of half-time at Millmoor to give Swindon a 3-1 win against Rotherham United in Division Three. The forward would finish the season with 11 goals in 21 matches. The victory kept Swindon in contention for promotion back into the Second Division under manager Bobby Smith.

MONDAY 24TH FEBRUARY 1997

Steve McMahon spent £400,000 on a player in his own image, bringing in the highly combative central midfielder Darren Bullock from Huddersfield Town. Things started well, with Bullock scoring less than 15 minutes into his debut, a 3-1 victory over Birmingham City. Swindon then suffered their traditional end-of-season McMahon slump, and Bullock won few friends when taking part in Huddersfield's end-of-season lap of honour in the final game of the campaign at the McAlpine Stadium. His popularity in Yorkshire was not recreated in Swindon. Over the next two seasons, Bullock would pick up 18 yellow cards and one red before being shipped off to Bury at a loss in January 1999 by new boss Jimmy Quinn.

TUESDAY 25TH FEBRUARY 1992

Steve Foley left Swindon Town for £50,000 to sign for Stoke City where he was reunited with his former boss Lou Macari. Foley would score 24 goals in 190 games after joining the club in the summer of 1987 from Sheffield United. A Scouser with a relaxed attitude to life, Foley had the habit of popping up with the occasional spectacular finish, most notably in the first leg of the play-off semi-finals at Blackburn Rovers in 1990 with a stunning volley from outside the penalty area.

FRIDAY 25TH FEBRUARY 1994

In a defining game in Swindon's Premiership season, Swindon moved into an early lead at Manchester City through Jan Age Fjortoft and then appeared to have a perfectly good second from the Norwegian ruled out for pushing. Town lost their way after that and eventually went down 2-1 after an own goal from Kevin Horlock and a low shot from David Rocastle.

THURSDAY 26TH FEBRUARY 1970

Swindon midfielder Fitzroy Simpson is born on this day in Trowbridge. Simpson would be an occasionally hot-headed midfielder who would also show bursts of skill. Simpson picked up two red cards in the first two months of the 1989/90 season and would be a substitute in the play-off final at Wembley. His ability was enough to earn him a move to the Premier League, when he joined Manchester City for £500,000 in March 1992 – another of the traditional sales of that era around deadline day. His finest hour came in 1998 when he played in the World Cup for Jamaica, having qualified through his parentage. Simpson started all three of Jamaica's group games.

SATURDAY 26TH FEBRUARY 1972

Swindon record their biggest win (to date) over Oxford United in a Division Two contest at the County Ground. Arthur Horsfield plundered a hat-trick against the visitors, while John Trollope also netted against Town's local rivals in a 4-0 rout. It's arguably one of the highlights of Dave Mackay's time in the manager's seat. Swindon finished above their local rivals in 11th place.

TUESDAY 27TH FEBRUARY 1968

Swindon enjoyed a dominant win over Grimsby Town, crushing their opponents 5-0 in a Division Three fixture in Wiltshire. Don Rogers and Pat Terry scored twice, while the final goal would come from a player who became much better known as a manager, with a certain Graham Taylor putting through his own net for the Mariners. It's the second time Swindon scored five in the league, but they failed to mount a serious push for promotion. In contrast, Grimsby dropped into Division Four at the season's end.

FRIDAY 27TH FEBRUARY 1995

Swindon brought in Andy Todd on loan from Middlesbrough as part of Steve McMahon's attempts to stave off consecutive relegations. The son of future manager Colin Todd failed to stop the rot, helping Town to just two wins in 13 games. Despite having a difficult time at Swindon, Todd would go on to have a decent career playing in the Premier League for Bolton Wanderers, Charlton Athletic, Blackburn Rovers and Derby County.

THURSDAY 28TH FEBRUARY 1974

The Swindon board have had enough and decide to dismiss manager Les Allen with the club bottom of the Second Division and relegation looking inevitable. Allen's last win is on New Year's Day, beating Preston North End. The crowd was just 2,600 for his final game in charge – a midweek home defeat by Luton Town. To be fair, this was an afternoon game to save power. With the financing of the new North Stand proving a crippling burden, Allen was always likely to find the job tough but not everyone found his assistant, Gordon Eddlestone, easy to work with. Allen did bring in one or two useful players, notably striker Peter Eastoe (on loan) and the popular Will Dixon, but perhaps it says it all that his next managerial job was in Greece.

SATURDAY 28TH FEBRUARY 1987

Swindon scored a 1-0 victory over fellow promotion contenders Middlesbrough in a big game in Division Three at the County Ground. Steve White notched the only goal in the second half against a Boro defence consisting of Gary Pallister and Tony Mowbray. It's the second in a run of seven straight wins for Lou Macari's side, but despite that a sequence of late draws leaves them in third place, with AFC Bournemouth and Middlesbrough taking the two automatic promotion slots.

WEDNESDAY 29TH FEBRUARY 1956

Floodlights were used for the first time in a league match at the County Ground and for once they shone on Swindon in a dismal season in Division Three (South). Town beat Millwall 1-0 with the great Maurice Owen the man to score in front of a crowd of 6,864. The lights had been initially put in place almost five years earlier, but Portsmouth's Fratton Park staged the first competitive floodlit match one week earlier.

SATURDAY 29TH FEBRUARY 1964

Swindon lost 4-1 at Newcastle United in their first-ever trip to St. James' Park in a Division Two fixture during the club's first season at the higher level. Town have fared little better there in seven subsequent attempts. Bobby Woodruff, one of Bert Head's prodigies, got the Swindon goal.

SWINDON TOWN
On This Day

MARCH

WEDNESDAY 1st MARCH 1933

It's the last-ever Swindon goal for David 'Harry' Morris in a Town shirt as he nets in the 2-2 draw with Southend United in Division Three (South). Morris' final total of 215 league goals and 229 in total remains a club record that is unlikely to be matched in an era where players are much more transient creatures. Morris, by all accounts, was a predator who did his best work inside the penalty box, with his first 100 goals scored at the rate of more than one per game. For seven seasons the solution to most Swindon problems was: "Give it to Morris!" before he was let go at the age of 35.

SATURDAY 1st MARCH 1947

Young striker Maurice Owen continued to underline his potential by scoring four goals as Swindon demolished Mansfield Town 6-1 in Division Three (South). Owen was in his first season with the club after being spotted playing for non-league Abingdon Town and was already being marked as 'one to watch' after a debut hat-trick. The striker, a tremendous header of the ball, would eventually go on to earn England 'B' honours.

FRIDAY 2nd MARCH 1962

Manager Bert Head continued with his policy of blooding players brought up through the club youth system in a Division Three (South) match at Reading, by giving 18-year-old Roger Smart his debut in place of the injured Keith Morgan. Smart helped Swindon to a 1-1 draw at Elm Park. Though he would be used sparingly over the next 18 months or so, Smart would grow into a first-team regular who would grab some of the most important goals in the club's history. He netted the winner that sent the club up into Division Two for the first time, plus the wonderfully scruffy opener in the 1969 League Cup Final at Wembley.

SATURDAY 2nd MARCH 1963

Swindon scored a memorable come-from-behind win against Bristol City en route to promotion. Trailing 2-0 at the hour mark, an Ernie Hunt penalty and a goal from Mike Summerbee levelled things up before Jack Smith scored the winner with nine minutes to go.

SUNDAY 2ND MARCH 1980

Swindon paid a club-record £150,000 to Southampton for their FA Cup-winning full-back David Peach. He signed as the replacement for John Trollope and had some big shoes to fill. His arrival was designed to help Swindon get back into the Second Division, with promotion still a possibility after the run to the League Cup semi-finals. Peach's arrival coincided with a bad run – coincidence or not – and his signing, along with Glenn Cockerill, seemed to alter the balance of the dressing room. Two years later, Peach was out of the door and on his way to Leyton Orient with the club facing the drop into Division Four.

SATURDAY 3RD MARCH 1979

Bobby Smith's side ran riot against Lincoln City in Division Three, recording a 6-0 win at the County Ground. The biggest victory of the season saw five different scorers. Strikers Andy Rowland (2) and Alan Mayes were predictably on target, with the other goals coming from Ray McHale, Ian Miller and substitute Chic Bates.

SATURDAY 3RD MARCH 1990

Swindon scored a comprehensive 3-0 win over Port Vale in Division Two, with the match remembered for an amazing goal from Colin Calderwood. The centre-back lobbed goalkeeper Mark Grew with a free kick that was no more than ten yards inside the Port Vale half, with the ball going in off the underside of the bar. The goal seemed to knock the heart out of Vale. Midway through the first half, Steve White took advantage of some hesitant defending to make it 2-0, then the Vale defence foolishly left space for Duncan Shearer to score the third before the break. The win left Swindon in third, five points behind Sheffield United.

TUESDAY 4TH MARCH 1980

David Peach's debut failed to go to plan as Swindon lose 6-2 at Millwall in Division Three. In a chaotic game, both sides put through their own net. Defender Billy Tucker opened the scoring for the Lions on ten minutes and Swindon find themselves 4-1 down by half-time.

SATURDAY 5TH MARCH 1910

Southern League Swindon beat the might of Manchester City to make the FA Cup semi-finals for the first time. A goal each from Bob Jefferson and Archie Bown, in front of a crowd of 14,429 fans, meant Town were just one step away from the final.

THURSDAY 5TH MARCH 1964

Manager Bert Head broke the club transfer record, with Swindon paying Northampton Town £10,000 for striker Frank Large – the first time Swindon had handed over a five-figure fee for a player. Things start well, with Large scoring twice on his debut to help Swindon to a 2-1 win over Plymouth Argyle. The win ends a sticky spell in Town's first season in Division Two – it's a first victory in eight games. But the deal quickly goes sour – Large would score just twice more and after seven blank games at the start of the next season, he was sold to Carlisle United in September.

FRIDAY 6TH MARCH 1964

It soon became obvious where the money for Frank Large came from, as Swindon sold Bobby Woodruff to First Division Wolverhampton Wanderers for £35,000, another club record. The wing-half is the first of Bert Head's carefully nurtured group of youngsters to leave the club. Woodruff scored 20 goals in 205 games and also had a valuable long throw. After leaving Wolves, he would go on to play for Crystal Palace, Cardiff City and Newport County. He also pursued one of the more interesting career choices for an ex-pro, going on to become a social worker.

WEDNESDAY 6TH MARCH 1974

Swindon announced the man they had chosen to replace the sacked Les Allen, with the club cut adrift at the bottom of Division Two. The board choose to go back to the future, with League Cup-winning manager Danny Williams returning to the County Ground for a second spell. The return of Williams at least brought back a little enthusiasm from fans, although the team were cut too far adrift at the foot of the table for any realistic thoughts of an escape from relegation.

MONDAY 7TH MARCH 1988

Swindon paid £25,000 to bring left-back Paul Bodin down the M4 from Newport County as Town looked for cover for first-choice left-back Phil King. After a modest start, Bodin grew into a successful, attacking full-back, playing in the 1990 and 1993 play-off finals – where he scored the crucial penalty. He also proved a profitable buy in other ways. After being sold to Crystal Palace for £550,000 in March 1991, he was bought back for half the price ten months later! His time as a player ended on a high as part of the Division Two championship squad. After spells in non-league management, 'Zippy' is now part of the youth-team coaching set-up at the County Ground.

TUESDAY 7TH MARCH 2000

Swindon, cut adrift at the foot of Division One, ended a club record of 19 league games without a victory by beating Huddersfield Town 2-0 at the County Ground. Lee Collins opened the scoring early and Town were able to hang on after the sending off of Dean Gorre. Chris Hay's stoppage-time penalty wrapped things up to bring a first victory of the new millennium! The previous win had been a 2-1 home success over Port Vale on October 26th 1999.

SATURDAY 8TH MARCH 1952

Swindon suffered their worst-ever Football League defeat, losing 9-0 at Torquay United in Division Three (South). There were extenuating circumstances, with goalkeeper Norman Uprichard taken off with concussion after an early collision. Left-back Harry May replaced him in goal – this is in the days before any subs were allowed. Later Uprichard reappeared, but as an outfield passenger as the goals rained in.

WEDNESDAY 8TH MARCH 1995

Swindon, hit by injuries, failed to hold on to their first-leg lead against Bolton Wanderers in the League Cup semi-finals. Jan Age Fjortoft finished from close range in the second half to give Steve McMahon's side a 3-1 aggregate lead, but a patched-up defence including Eddie Murray and Adrian Viveash can't stop a Bolton comeback, which is completed by the never popular John McGinlay. Bolton won 3-1, and 4-3 on aggregate to go to Wembley.

SATURDAY 9TH MARCH 1912

Southern League champions Swindon beat Everton 2-1 to make the semi-finals of the FA Cup for the second time in three seasons. Bob Jefferson and Archie Bown are the scorers in what is the club's last win over Everton to date.

TUESDAY 9TH MARCH 1976

Swindon drew 1-1 with Rotherham United in Division Three in a game that turned out to be the last appearance for one of the 1969 League Cup winners – Joe Butler. Brought in by Danny Williams for £5,500 from Newcastle United in 1965, Butler would be transformed by a move from right-back to midfield and was a steady contributor to the cause for the next decade. Always reliable for a couple of goals a season, Butler would end up making 428 Swindon appearances, putting him eighth in the all-time list.

SATURDAY 10TH MARCH 2001

Swindon paid what proved to be their final visit to Oxford United's Manor Ground and it turned out to be a successful and important one. Two volleys from Steve Robinson helped Town to a 2-0 win in Division Two, with Oxford reduced to nine men for the last 25 minutes. It completed a league double over the old rivals and the wins were vital as Swindon stayed up by one point. Oxford, meanwhile, finished bottom, conceding 100 league goals.

THURSDAY 11TH MARCH 1993

As was so often the case in the 1990s, the arrival of the transfer deadline sees a player sold to balance the books. This time it's full-back David Kerslake who heads out the door. After four successful seasons, he joins Premier League Leeds United for £500,000.

SATURDAY 11TH MARCH 2000

Swindon, stuck at the bottom of Division One, caused a huge surprise by beating the league leaders Charlton Athletic 1-0 at The Valley with an early Steve Cowe goal. At the time, 54 points separated the sides at the top and bottom of the table, while the London side had won 12 straight league games going into the contest.

SATURDAY 12TH MARCH 1983

Swindon manager John Trollope came under increasing pressure from fans after a last-minute home defeat by Chester City. The result meant it was now five games without a win and hopes of immediate promotion back out of Division Four were receding. Andy Rowland and Paul Rideout had both scored to put Swindon back into the game, but John Thomas' second saw all three points head back north

SATURDAY 13TH MARCH 1993

Swindon beat top-of-the-table Newcastle United 2-1 in a high quality Division One contest. After trailing at the break, Paul Bodin scored a penalty six minutes into the second half. Shortly afterwards, Colin Calderwood steamed in to score from a corner meaning Swindon took four points off Kevin Keegan's eventual champions.

FRIDAY 13TH MARCH 1998

Swindon paid £120,000 for some punch up front by signing Iffy Onuora from Gillingham. The likeable Scot proved to be an effective target man, scoring on his debut and then getting 20 goals the following season under Jimmy Quinn. Onuora would eventually head back to Gillingham as the financial problems at the club got worse. After being brought back to the club by Andy King to work with the club's youngsters, Onuora ended up replacing him as manager when King was dismissed but couldn't quite do enough to prevent relegation into the football basement during his spell in charge, despite being a popular figure with the hardcore of fans left.

SATURDAY 14TH MARCH 1981

Swindon striker Sam Parkin was born on this day in Roehampton. For three seasons, Parkin would be a prolific centre forward, with his partnership with Tommy Mooney firing Swindon into the play-offs in 2004. Parkin started life with a hat-trick on his debut and never really stopped scoring. The forward earned a call-up to the Scotland 'futures' side during his time in Wiltshire and ended up with 73 goals in just 142 appearances. Sadly a broken ankle following his move to Ipswich Town seems to have robbed him of the spark seen at the County Ground.

SATURDAY MARCH 15TH 1969

It's the greatest day in the history of Swindon Town. Danny Williams' side overcame the Wembley mud, and Arsenal's late comeback, to win the League Cup and earn the club a first major honour. Swindon look set to win 1-0 as Roger Smart ran the ball in following some chaotic defending, with goalkeeper Peter Downsborough apparently in unbeatable form. That changed just four minutes from time, as Bobby Gould gets to a pass just before the keeper to equalise. Swindon still pass and play in extra time. Don Rogers scored once as Arsenal can't deal with the pressure from a corner and he ends the match in perfect style. As Arsenal push forward, Swindon counter, and 'The Don' races free to round international keeper Bob Wilson with apparent nonchalance to complete a 3-1 win. The bare facts of the game fail to do an amazing run to the final – and the Wembley performance – justice.

SATURDAY 15TH MARCH 1986

Swindon beat Burnley 3-1 in Division Four, creating a new club record of 14 home league wins in a row. The players had equalled the record back in January, but bad weather meant a succession of postponements. On a nervous day, Charlie Henry volleyed home the opening goal, but David Cole's short back-header let the Clarets back into the game with Les Lawrence being handed an easy finish. Swindon improved in the second half after Dave Bamber nods in Leigh Barnard's corner, before Colin Gordon's full-length header late on establishes the new record. In a rather bizarre postscript among the celebrations, the Burnley coach departs without defender Jim Heggarty and manager Lou Macari phones the police to get them to turn back and collect him.

TUESDAY 16TH MARCH 2010

Swindon record their first-ever Football League victory on this date, beating Southampton at St. Mary's Stadium. Charlie Austin, who had started the season playing non-league football along the south coast at Poole, rounded Kelvin Davis for the only goal of the game and Town survived the late sending off of Simon Ferry to hold on for three points.

WEDNESDAY 17TH MARCH 1943

Swindon forward Roger Hunt, universally known as 'Ernie', was born in the town on this day. Hunt would be the youngest player to break through into the first team when making his debut age 16, having been discovered while working for British Rail. Hunt scored 27 goals to help Swindon into Division Two, but a variety of ailments, including tonsillitis, appendicitis and a broken foot, meant he missed some key games in the 1964/65 season, where Swindon slid back down into Division Three. Early into the new season, he followed Bobby Woodruff to Wolves. Hunt would finish with 88 goals in 237 Swindon games and earn nationwide notoriety for the famous 'donkey drop' goal for Coventry, where the ball was flicked up from a free kick for him to volley home.

SATURDAY 17TH MARCH 1962

Swindon pay a first-ever visit to Bradford Park Avenue in the Football League in Division Three, with the match ending in a 2-2 draw at the Horton Park Avenue ground. With Swindon leading 2-1 with goals from Jack Smith and Arnold Darcy, Jock Buchanan scored for the Yorkshire side with just two minutes remaining. Ernie Hunt played on his 19th birthday.

SATURDAY 18TH MARCH 1939

Swindon came out on top against Reading in a Division Three (South) local derby at the County Ground. Town won 4-2 with striker Ben Morton scoring his 27th goal of the season.

SATURDAY 19TH MARCH 1994

Swindon defy expectations by holding Manchester United to a 2-2 draw in the Premier League at the County Ground. A game full of drama featured the sending off of Eric Cantona for a blatant stamp on John Moncur as Town twice conjured up equalisers. After falling behind early, Swindon score when Luc Nijholt's shot takes a giant deflection. Paul Ince restored apparent normality before Cantona's dismissal. The second came two minutes from time as Jan Age Fjortoft finally forced home following efforts from Adrian Whitbread and Keith Scott.

SUNDAY 19TH MARCH 1995

Trailing 2-1 with 16 minutes left at The Hawthorns, Swindon produced a spectacular comeback to beat West Bromwich Albion 5-2 in a televised Division One encounter. The revival is started by Jan Age Fjortoft, who scored his final goal in Swindon colours. Peter Thorne then runs riot, completing a hat-trick in front of the travelling support, while Ty Gooden provided the crucial third. The win revives Swindon hopes of avoiding a second successive relegation.

TUESDAY 20TH MARCH 1984

A strong Swindon side earn some silverware – the Wiltshire FA Centenary Cup! But Town do need a penalty shoot-out to beat non-league Trowbridge in the final. Swindon eventually came through 4-3, despite missing two of their first three spot kicks, with Alan Mayes and Gary Emmanuel at fault. Trowbridge had a similar failure of nerve, and the shoot-out ended when Scott Enderbsy kept out Stuart Ashton's effort in sudden death.

MONDAY 21ST MARCH 1983

Swindon decided to sack John Trollope as manager. The board swung the axe following demonstrations by fans after a home defeat by Darlington the previous Saturday in Division Four. The supporters' demands changed after seeing the side take just one point from the previous 21 available – with the fact that it was a club legend in charge making no difference. His job had been made increasingly difficult by working with a tiny budget, forcing him to bring through youth-system players and rely on inexperienced free transfers. In addition, there was also the expectation of an immediate promotion, simply because Swindon had never been in the basement division before. Trollope had subsequently admitted that he found it difficult dealing with senior players – and that he felt let down by some of them during his time in charge. His ambivalence to taking the role in the first place meant he was able to activate a clause in his contract allowing him to return to the youth-team role. The assistant Trollope appointed, striker Ken Beamish, is given the caretaker's job and a chance to prove himself.

MONDAY 22ND MARCH 1999

Swindon agreed to loan Jimmy Glass out to Carlisle United, who were without a recognised senior keeper through injury as they try and avoid relegation out of the Football League. Glass scored the injury-time winner against Plymouth on the final day of the season that saves the Cumbrians and relegates Scarborough.

MONDAY 22ND MARCH 2004

Swindon announced plans to leave their County Ground home and move to a new ground, to be built on Shaw Tip in the west of town. The plans presented to the press included a new 22,000 all-seater stadium, plus a hotel and a gym to help raise funds for the club. The hope is to complete the new ground in time for the 2007/08 season. The club make the plans public before applying for planning permission and they quickly face protests from local residents and environmental campaigners.

THURSDAY 22ND MARCH 2007

With Swindon outside of the top three in League Two, manager Paul Sturrock goes wild on transfer deadline day, bringing in four new signings to go with the earlier capture of striker Barry Corr. Sturrock signed the Manchester City striker Ashley Grimes, Nottingham Forest forward Kevin James, Bristol City centre-back David Partridge and French defender Claude Gnapka. Gnapka and Partridge never featured, while Grimes and James just made sporadic appearances from the subs' bench.

THURSDAY 23RD MARCH 1995

Cult striker Jan Age Fjortoft departed the County Ground on transfer deadline day. While the news is depressing enough with Town fighting relegation, the fee for the forward, £1.3m, is met with widespread fury, though manager Steve McMahon insists Middlesbrough's offer was the only one on the table and had to be accepted. To add to the perversity of the deal, £340,000 of the money was spent on a left-back, the hapless Jason Drysdale. Predictably, Swindon struggled for goals in their remaining games and suffer relegation for the second season in a row.

SATURDAY 24TH MARCH 1979

Andy Rowland and Alan Mayes worked in perfect tandem as Swindon scored a 4-1 win over Tranmere Rovers in a Division Three match at the County Ground. The pair both got on the score-sheet – Rowland twice and Mayes once – with Ray McHale netting the other goal. Rovers' centre-half John Williams, who made his debut that day, admitted the pair gave him a real football education.

TUESDAY 24TH MARCH 1987

Lou Macari's side look on course for back-to-back promotions as they make it seven league wins on the spin by beating Bolton Wanderers 2-0 in Division Three. Steve White opened the scoring while Mark Jones wrapped up the win with a penalty just after the hour.

TUESDAY 24TH MARCH 2009

Simon Cox scored his third hat-trick of the season as Swindon bagged a vital 4-2 win over Northampton Town in a League One game at Sixfields. After Swindon went a goal down, Cox scored with a header from Anthony McNamee's cross, then produced an effortless lob from Billy Paynter's through ball for his second. Paynter was then set up by Cox to make it 3-1. After the Cobblers pull a goal back, Cox chested in Paynter's perfect cross. The game finished 4-3 and it meant that Cox became the first Swindon player to score three hat-tricks in a season since 1947 after scoring three against Hartlepool United and Scunthorpe United.

WEDNESDAY 25TH MARCH 1936

The chance of silverware looked to go west after Swindon were beaten 2-0 at home by Coventry City in the first leg of the Division Three (South) Cup Final. A crowd of 3,610 give up their afternoons to be there. Coventry go on to clinch the competition 5-2 on aggregate.

TUESDAY 25TH MARCH 1986

Swindon signed Manchester United's young keeper Fraser Digby on loan. Although he doesn't play a senior game before going back to Old Trafford he catches the eye of manager Lou Macari…

SATURDAY 26TH MARCH 1910

Swindon travelled to White Hart Lane to take on Newcastle United in the FA Cup semi-final. A crowd of 33,000 are in attendance to see if the Southern League side can upset the First Division Magpies and make the final. The defining moment came at 0-0, when Freddy Wheatcroft hit the post. Not long after, two goals in three minutes from Newcastle ensured there would be no upset and a memorable FA Cup run was over.

SATURDAY 26TH MARCH 1983

Caretaker manager Ken Beamish took charge of Swindon for the first time in a Division Four contest at York City. They emerged with a creditable 0-0 draw against a side still in with a chance of promotion.

MONDAY 27TH MARCH 1899

Future Swindon manager Louis Page was born on this day in Kirkdale on Merseyside. Page, an England international in football and baseball, was given the difficult task of managing the club in the immediate aftermath of World War II. Page stayed with the club until the end of the 1952/53 season, when the board decided to dismiss him after four years finishing in the bottom half of Division Three (South).

FRIDAY MARCH 27TH 1992

Swindon sell top scorer Duncan Shearer to play-off rivals Blackburn Rovers for £800,000. 'The Postman' departed with 32 goals to his name. In his absence, Swindon can't manage more than one goal in any game on the run-in and so miss out on a place in the end-of-season play-offs. Shearer's replacement, the Wimbledon striker Terry Gibson, scored just once in his loan spell. In contrast, Blackburn, fresh with Jack Walker's millions to spend, squeeze into sixth and win promotion, with Shearer scoring one goal in six games before being sold in the summer to Aberdeen. The suspicion remains, to this day, that Blackburn's deal to sign Shearer was more about depriving Swindon of his goals than seeing a long-term future for him at Ewood Park. Eventually, Shearer goes on to earn long overdue international honours, winning seven caps for Scotland and domestically, the Scottish League Cup.

WEDNESDAY 27th MARCH 2002

It's confirmed that Swindon go into administration for the second time, with outgoing phone lines from the County Ground cut off and the PFA assisting in paying the players' wages. The administrators insist that there is sufficient money for the club to at least play out the season. The collapse of ITV Digital is partly blamed. The administrators say that the club needs to move to flourish, with Hacker Young insisting: "It is quite clear that the future of Swindon Town football club lies in a property deal that takes them away from the County Ground."

THURSDAY 28th MARCH 1996

Manager Steve McMahon spends £100,000 on bringing diminutive striker Steve Cowe to the club from Aston Villa. He scored one goal in the end-of-season run in – in the 3-1 win at Chesterfield – which clinches the Division Two title. Cowe would go on to score 12 goals in total in more than 100 appearances, many of which came from the subs' bench.

SATURDAY 29th MARCH 1969

Swindon and Watford met in what turned out to be a shoot-out for the Division Three title, with a crowd of 28,898 squeezing into the County Ground. It's Watford who came out winners with a late goal from Barry Endean – the only home league defeat of the season. Even though Swindon would remain unbeaten for the rest of the campaign, Watford went on to take the title on goal average thanks to that victory.

SATURDAY 30th MARCH 1912

Swindon drew 0-0 with Barnsley in an FA Cup semi-final at Stamford Bridge to earn a replay, but at a heavy cost. England international Harold Fleming took a battering from the Tykes, with a groin injury ruling him out for months afterwards.

MONDAY 30th MARCH 1992

Swindon paid £80,000 to sign midfielder John Moncur from Tottenham reserves. Moncur proved to be a high quality midfielder, shining in the Premier League where he was the club's Player of the Season before signing for West Ham for £1m.

SATURDAY 30TH MARCH 2002

Swindon fans enjoyed putting one over old boss Steve McMahon as he returned to the County Ground with Blackpool. Youth system product Alan Young scored the only goal of the game in a Division Two fixture, keeping Town in a thoroughly mid-table 14th position.

TUESDAY 30TH MARCH 2004

Swindon produced a superb comeback to get a point at Port Vale in Division Two. Town were trailing 3-0 after an hour – Billy Paynter had opened the scoring for Vale. The physical presence of Rory Fallon changed the game when he came on at half-time as Swindon adopted a direct style to get back into the contest. With Fallon causing mayhem, Sam Parkin and Matt Hewlett scored, before Fallon completed a superb comeback by chesting in the equaliser. Swindon finished the season in the play-off places on the final day after their draw with Hartlepool, with Port Vale missing out in seventh place.

MONDAY 31ST MARCH 1975

Striker Peter Eastoe scored his 25th goal of the season as Swindon drew 1-1 at Dean Court with AFC Bournemouth in Division Three. It marked the end of a run of one win in 10 games that would ultimately cost Swindon a chance of an immediate return to Division Two.

SUNDAY 31ST MARCH 1991

Ossie Ardiles' departure to Newcastle United as manager is revealed, ironically 24 hours after Swindon beat a managerless Newcastle 3-2 at the County Ground. Ardiles has seen two of his back four sold in the previous month, with Jon Gittens (Southampton) and Paul Bodin (Crystal Palace) leaving the County Ground to bring in almost £1m in much needed revenue. Chief executive Peter Day insists to fans that there was little chance of keeping Ardiles at the club, saying: "Once a person has made up his mind to leave there is little you can do to try and persuade them otherwise. We asked him if it was about money and quite clearly it wasn't." It is a big blow with Swindon, like Newcastle, struggling to avoid the drop into Division Three and a game with struggling West Bromwich Albion to come.

SWINDON TOWN
On This Day

APRIL

MONDAY 1st APRIL 1991

Swindon, without a manager following Ossie Ardiles' departure, saw their relegation worries increase after a 2-1 defeat by West Bromwich Albion at The Hawthorns. Swindon had taken the lead through Paul Rideout, with what would be his final goal for the club. He'd been brought back for a loan spell from Southampton just before Ardiles joined Newcastle United. Steve Parkin and Graham Roberts, with a second-half penalty, earned the Baggies victory.

MONDAY 1st APRIL 2002

Richard McKinney played his only game for Swindon. The Ulsterman replaced Bart Griemink in goal in a 2-0 defeat at Stoke City's Britannia Stadium in Division Two. McKinney spent just the one season with Swindon after being signed from Manchester City.

THURSDAY 1st APRIL 2010

Local newspaper the *Swindon Advertiser* claims that Swindon were to trial an "Extra Definition" way to watch matches at the County Ground. Fans will be given special glasses to wear as is the norm for 3D films, with the kit enhanced with a special layer of material so supporters wearing the glasses will feel right in the middle of the action. If the date of publication isn't a give-away, the name of the manufacturers of the glasses L'Aproolif surely is – it's an anagram of April Fool.

SATURDAY 2nd APRIL 1927

Swindon played their final league game with Aberdare Athletic in Division Three (South). A brace from Charlie Jeffries and a goal from Bertie Denyer was enough to see off the Welsh side 3-2. Aberdare would only record one victory over Swindon in 12 meetings before failing to earn re-election.

MONDAY 2nd APRIL 1951

The first-ever floodlit game is staged at the County Ground after Swindon paid £350 to get the lights installed. More than 3,000 supporters turned up to see the novelty despite persistent rain. Bristol City are good enough to provide the opposition, and they also do the decent thing by losing 2-1, with Scottish winger William Millar scoring a goal in each half.

SATURDAY 2ND APRIL 1963

Swindon and Bradford Park Avenue cross swords for the last time in the Football League. Jack Smith and John Stevens scored in the second half to earn Town a 2-1 victory as they chased an elusive first-ever promotion from Division Three. Both sides went the opposite way at the end of the season as Swindon headed up, and Park Avenue down. The Yorkshire side never reached the heights of Division Three again. They would go on to drop out of the league in 1970 after failing to win re-election.

TUESDAY 2ND APRIL 1985

Striker Barry Corr was born in Newcastle, County Wicklow, Ireland. A tall forward, Corr was an invaluable loan signing by Paul Sturrock in the 2006/07 season, scoring on his debut in a key win at Lincoln City and adding a physical dimension up front. Corr, already hampered by problems with the vertebrae in his back, would then go on to suffer increasingly with shoulder injuries. Sadly, it would mean he would only play a limited role in the next two seasons before being released in the summer of 2009.

SATURDAY 3RD APRIL 1909

History is made as Harold Fleming became the first – and so far only – Swindon Town player to represent England. Fleming, and England, beat Scotland 2-0 at Crystal Palace in front of 40,000 supporters. It's an amazing achievement having made his first-team debut less than 18 months prior, in October 1907, with Swindon still playing in the Southern League.

WEDNESDAY 3RD APRIL 1912

The absence of two key players proved costly as Swindon were beaten 1-0 by Barnsley in their FA Cup semi-final replay at Meadow Lane. Harold Fleming, injured in the original match, sat the game out along with Billy Tout, the regular penalty taker. When Swindon got a first-half penalty, Archie Bown stepped up but his spot-kick was saved by the Barnsley keeper Jack Cooper. Phil Bratley scored in the second half to put Barnsley into the final, and Swindon have never been as close to lifting the FA Cup since.

SATURDAY 3RD APRIL 2010

Swindon recorded a first-ever win at Elland Road – and it was an emphatic one as they beat Leeds United 3-0 to move into second place in League One. Billy Paynter scored twice, including one superb effort from outside of the penalty area, while Charlie Austin added a third with more than half an hour to play.

SATURDAY 4TH APRIL 1914

As would happen half a century later, a 'D. Rogers' starred at the County Ground. On this occasion though, it's Dave Rogers, who scored four times in a 5-0 win over Portsmouth in the Southern League – on his debut! Rogers would be back with Swindon after World War I, playing in the club's inaugural Football League fixture, with his last game for the club coming in 1926, a win over Newport County.

THURSDAY 4TH APRIL 1991

Swindon appointed Glenn Hoddle as manager after the abrupt departure of Ossie Ardiles. Hoddle, just 33, returned to English football from Monaco, appointing John Gorman as assistant. Hoddle described his arrival as a "new adventure" and the board back him, giving him a three-year contract to prove himself as Town continued along the route of giving big-name players a first chance in management. Fans hoping to see Hoddle put on a red shirt look likely to be disappointed, with Hoddle saying that a chronic knee injury means he's unlikely to play. His management proves shrewd enough to keep Swindon in the Second Division.

SATURDAY 4TH APRIL 1998

Swindon goalkeeper Fraser Digby became only the third player to rack up 500 games for the club after striker Maurice Owen and full-back John Trollope. The match itself was a bit of a let down as Digby failed to get the clean sheet he wants with Swindon beaten 1-0 by Charlton Athletic at the County Ground in Division One. Digby reached a grand total of 505 matches before a disagreement with Steve McMahon would lead to his departure. Digby was at the club in six promotion-winning seasons in total (including 1989/90) although he didn't appear in the 1985/86 campaign.

FRASER DIGBY: ONE OF THE MORE MEMORABLE OF 505 FIRST-TEAM GAMES

SATURDAY 5TH APRIL 1913

Swindon players lined up on opposing sides in the England versus Scotland Home International at Stamford Bridge. Forward Harold Fleming played for England, while defender Jock Walker was part of the Scotland side. Fleming enjoyed the day more, as England won 1-0 in front of 52,500 fans.

FRIDAY 5TH APRIL 1985

It's announced that Swindon have decided to sack manager Lou Macari and assistant manager Harry Gregg, less than a season after they arrived at the club via a sponsorship deal from Lowndes Lambert. Chairman Brian Hillier cites the pair's relationship as the problem, saying they have shown an "inability to work together". The board eventually decided to act when they feel Macari and Gregg cannot resolve their differences, with the directors insisting the pair have been given enough opportunities to deal with any conflict. There are even allegations, not confirmed by the club, that Gregg has been keeping diaries documenting Macari's activities. Macari's sacking is only narrowly approved by the board, by four votes to three, but it hugely angers supporters, who can see signs of progress under his leadership.

WEDNESDAY 5TH APRIL 1995

Swindon lost 1-0 at home to Bolton Wanderers in Division One to slip closer to relegation. Player-manager Steve McMahon was sent off for a crunching first-half challenge by referee Graham Barber. At half-time it prompts tannoy announcer Peter Lewis to venture an opinion to the crowd that "I've seen some crap refereeing decisions in my time but…" While the fans respond to his comments with amusement, club management are less indulging and he is promptly escorted from the premises. An 89th-minute goal from Bolton's Alan Thompson completes the evening's entertainment.

TUESDAY 6TH APRIL 1915

Archie Bown became the first – and so far only – Swindon player to score six goals in a game. Bown netted all six as Swindon beat Watford 6-0 in the Southern League. The score-line is all the more surprising as Watford would go on to clinch the Southern League title. The victory is Swindon's last win before football is suspended for World War I.

TUESDAY 6TH APRIL 1976

Swindon scored an important Division Three win to increase their chances of escaping relegation into Division Four for the first time. Town won 2-1 at Colchester United's Layer Road ground with a Trevor Anderson penalty and a goal from Dave Syrett. Seven years on, there are still three League Cup winners in the side, Don Rogers, John Trollope and Frank Burrows.

SATURDAY 6TH APRIL 1985

Fans get their first opportunity to vent their feelings about the sacking of Lou Macari, as Swindon host Southend United in Division Four. They do so with great vigour. Fans chant Macari's name and there are also pitch invasions in protest at his dismissal. There is one hint that things could change though – with Macari attending the game – while Harry Gregg does not. With John Trollope in caretaker charge, the team are focused enough to win 2-0 with goals from Garry Nelson and Colin Gordon in front of 2,693 fans.

FRIDAY 6TH APRIL 1990

Brian Hillier's decision to appeal against his ban from football backfires. Having been suspended for backing Swindon to lose against Newcastle United, Hillier received a six-month suspension from the game extended to three years by the Football Association.

SATURDAY 7TH APRIL 1990

With Fraser Digby and Nicky Hammond both missing, on-loan goalkeeper Kevin Dearden made his one and only Swindon appearance in a Division Two match at AFC Bournemouth. Although Dearden, signed from Spurs, was beaten by a Luther Blissett effort just before half-time, goals from Fitzroy Simpson and Jon Gittens give Swindon a 2-1 win. Dearden would become a loan specialist during his time at Spurs, being sent out to nine different clubs, Swindon included, before signing for Brentford.

WEDNESDAY 8TH APRIL 1908

Swindon outside-left William 'Bud' Flanagan was born. He scored three goals in 45 games in the 1933/34 and 1934/35 seasons, having been signed from Bath City for £50. The closest he came to the dream partnership was when Alan Fowler was up front...

TUESDAY 8TH APRIL 1986

Lou Macari's Swindon side sealed promotion from Division Four by beating Chester City 4-2 in a fiery encounter in front of a crowd of 12,630. Bruising striker Steve Johnson scored early for Chester, with Dave Bamber equalising with a header before half-time. Then came a Chester penalty which Johnson scored twice – the first time it was disallowed for encroachment. However, Swindon applied serious pressure after the break. Bamber headed in his second, then 60 seconds later Peter Coyne's cross cuts out the keeper and allows Bryan Wade to make it 3-2 with a far-post finish. Leigh Barnard would get the fourth to make the game safe but there was still time for Chris Kamara to be knocked out by an elbow and Coyne to have his penalty saved. A pitch invasion followed at full time. Keeper Kenny Allen said he'd never played in an atmosphere like it, with manager Macari still setting new targets afterwards, saying: "Never in a month of Sundays did I think we'd be in this position – but we'd all kick ourselves if we didn't win the championship now."

MONDAY 8TH APRIL 1996

Swindon continued their progress to the Division Two title with a 2-0 win at Crewe Alexandra courtesy of goals from Kevin Horlock and on-loan David Preece. It was Preece's only goal in a seven-game loan spell from Derby County. Preece died in 2007, aged just 44. At his peak he won England B caps.

TUESDAY 9TH APRIL 1985

Swindon fans stepped up the pressure on the board to reinstate manager Lou Macari. An Action Group is formed to campaign for his return, while a petition carrying 1,500 signatures is presented to club officials at the County Ground.

MONDAY 9TH APRIL 2007

Swindon scored a vital 2-1 victory over Torquay United at the County Ground in League Two. After Blair Sturrock netted early, Torquay won a penalty with eight minutes left that was calmly converted by Lee Thorpe. The Devon fans had barely sat down from their celebrations when youngster Lukas Jutkiewicz, on as a sub, fired in the winner.

WEDNESDAY 10TH APRIL 1985

Fan power wins as the board voted unanimously to bring Lou Macari back to the club as manager, though his former number two Harry Gregg did not return. Instead, Macari asks John Trollope to step up from his role with the youth team. Chairman Brian Hillier describes the whole saga as "a traumatic time" while Macari says returning to the club is like coming "back home". Macari has been out of work for five days. The board insist his return follows a full consideration of the facts and is not down to the fans' obvious displeasure.

SATURDAY 10TH APRIL 2004

Swindon and Bristol City clash at the County Ground with both sides looking for promotion out of the Second Division. City took the lead through future Swindon player Christian Roberts just before half-time. The Swindon equaliser was nothing short of sensational. Substitute Rory Fallon flicked the ball up with his head on the edge of the penalty area before unleashing the perfect overhead kick that cannoned in off the underside of the crossbar to earn Swindon a point. The game finished 1-1 and both sides go on to make the play-offs.

SATURDAY 11TH APRIL 1987

Swindon won a knockabout local derby with Bristol Rovers by 4-3, with the game staged at Ashton Gate rather than the club's temporary home of Twerton Park in Bath. Swindon, in second, trailed 2-0 in the first half to a side struggling to avoid relegation. Goals from Steve White and Jimmy Quinn turned things round, only for Phil Purnell to make it 3-2 from a penalty given against Dave Hockaday. Dave Bamber's sharp turn and quality finish made it 3-3, then a minute later Jimmy Quinn volleyed home a corner that wasn't cleared to give Town victory.

SATURDAY 12TH APRIL 1902

Goalkeeper Ted Nash is born. Nash would go on to play 253 games for the club, spending the entire 1920s at Swindon. Nash was also wedded to the club in another sense, marrying the Swindon Ladies' keeper. A fine wicketkeeper, Nash's greatest moment arguably came in his final season, in a 2-0 FA Cup win at Manchester United.

MONDAY 12TH APRIL 1993

The miracle of St. Andrew's took place on Easter Monday as Swindon came from 4-1 down with half an hour to go to beat Birmingham City 6-4. Then Craig Maskell and Dave Mitchell got to work. With 14 minutes to go, the game had been completely transformed – it's 4-4 as Mitchell scored twice, one a diving header, and Maskell once. With 12 minutes to go, Maskell looped a beautiful header from a corner over Andy Gosney, before Mitchell rounded the sprawling keeper in injury time to complete his hat-trick and mark the end of a quite surreal match which completely defied analysis.

SATURDAY 13TH APRIL 1968

Swindon and Southport drew 3-3 at the County Ground in Division Three and it was a game the nation had beamed into their living rooms that night, as it formed part of *Match of the Day* – the first time the cameras had been to the County Ground. Swindon went 1-0 up early and trailed 3-2 at one stage, before Don Rogers, who was the focus of David Coleman's pre-match comments, scored in injury time to prompt a mini pitch invasion – in terms of numbers and size of invader.

SATURDAY 13TH APRIL 1974

With relegation inevitable, Town players and fans were cheered up a little by a surprise 1-0 win over Blackpool in Division Two. Tommy Jenkins, the man signed to 'replace' Don Rogers got the only goal. It's a first victory in 13 league games and gave Danny Williams a first win since his return to the club to replace Les Allen as manager.

SATURDAY 14TH APRIL 1970

Swindon, with an outside chance of snatching second place in Division Two, have any hopes of promotion to the top flight ended with a comprehensive home defeat by Middlesbrough. Swindon were beaten 3-0, their first home defeat in the league all season. The result, along with a draw at home to Blackpool the week before, means Swindon finish three points off second in the days when only the top two sides are promoted.

SATURDAY 15TH APRIL 1967

Swindon earned their second and final league win at Workington in Division Three. Town eased past the Cumbrian side 3-1 as Roger Smart, Willie Penman and Pat Terry all scored in front of a meagre 1,611 crowd. Workington finished bottom and their ongoing decline for the next decade had begun, ending with failure to be re-elected in 1977.

SATURDAY 15TH APRIL 1980

Andy Rowland has his career day. The striker scored four times as Swindon thrashed Rotherham United 6-2 at the County Ground in Division Three. The game is tight at the break at 2-1, with Rowland having only scored once. He then went on to bag three goals in 18 second-half minutes to put Swindon 5-1 ahead. Striker partner Alan Mayes has to join him and he gets number six, before the Millers pull one back with an 89th-minute penalty.

FRIDAY 16TH APRIL 1965

Swindon pulled off an important win against Rotherham United as they battled to stay in Division Two – but the win came at a cost. Ernie Hunt, rushed back from a broken foot, scored early on in the 3-2 victory over the Millers, but had to come off with another break that ruled him out for the rest of the season. Despite Hunt's absence, goals from Roger Smart and Mike Summerbee saw Town through to a much needed victory.

TUESDAY 16TH APRIL 1974

Swindon's relegation into Division Three was confirmed without kicking a ball. Town can't escape the bottom three after Crystal Palace beat Fulham 3-1. Palace followed Swindon down anyway.

TUESDAY 17TH APRIL 1984

With Swindon on course for their lowest-ever Football League finish under Ken Beamish, Town registered their lowest-ever Football League attendance at the County Ground. Leigh Barnard's winner against Darlington was witnessed by just 1,681 paying customers as Town's fight against an unhealthy spiral of a small budget lead to a lack of on-pitch success, leading to fewer fans going through the turnstiles.

TUESDAY 18TH APRIL 1911

Swindon won 3-2 against QPR at White Hart Lane in the Southern Charity Cup in an eternal cup tie. This match was a third replay, with Ivor Mabberley scoring late in normal time and then in extra time to put Swindon into the final. Bad light had stopped the previous replay!

SATURDAY 18TH APRIL 1987

Match of the Day is in Wiltshire again for the meeting of the two promotion contenders in Division Three. Swindon drew 1-1 with eventual champions AFC Bournemouth at the County Ground, with Barry Davies on hand to commentate on Swindon's equaliser – a free kick knocked down for Dave Hockaday to finish.

SATURDAY 19TH APRIL 1986

Around 2,000 Swindon supporters descended on Field Mill, the home of Mansfield Town, in expectation of Town clinching the Division Four title. They just needed one point to do so. Though Swindon went behind to a goal from Neville Chamberlain, it's joy in our time thanks to Leigh Barnard's equaliser ten minutes later. Fans and players mingle contentedly afterwards. Even though Town draw, it left the possibility of reaching the 100-point mark still within range. Mansfield would go on to join Town in Division Three, after finishing in third, 21 points behind Lou Macari's side.

SATURDAY 19TH APRIL 2008

Swindon enjoyed their biggest win under Maurice Malpas, as they shred a doomed Port Vale 6-0. Lee Peacock, Craig Easton, Jack Smith, Anthony McNamee, Michael Timlin and Ben Joyce score past debutant Vale keeper Chris Martin.

SATURDAY 20TH APRIL 1996

A 1-1 draw at second-place Blackpool was enough for Swindon to be able to celebrate immediate promotion back into Division One. Kevin Horlock's goal puts Swindon on their way, and though Andy Barlow drills in a long-range shot to level thing up in the second half, Town ease to the point they need after relegation the season before, while fans go on to enjoy a weekend at the seaside in some style. The result continues an outstanding season away from home, where Swindon would lose just three times.

SATURDAY 21ST APRIL 1979

Swindon and Watford draw a crowd of 16,414 to the County Ground with both sides looking to get into Division Two. Graham Taylor's side are beaten 2-0. The second goal, a well-constructed four-man move, earned high praise. Ian Miller fed John Trollope and his cross into the box was flicked on by Bryan Hamilton for Andy Rowland to volley in at almost full stretch. Barry Davies, at the County Ground for *Match of the Day*, was most impressed, describing it as "as good a goal as you will see in any division".

SATURDAY 22ND APRIL 1911

Swindon secured the Southern League title for the first time with a 3-0 win over the holders and their nearest rivals Brighton & Hove Albion. Billy Tout's retaken penalty, Freddy Wheatcroft's header from a corner and Harold Fleming's close-range finish saw Swindon run out comfortable winners in front of a crowd of 7,000 mostly damp supporters.

SATURDAY 23RD APRIL 1994

Swindon were beaten 4-2 at home by Wimbledon, with Town undone by a flurry of late goals. It meant relegation from the Premier League was now mathematically assured, although the reality was stark for some time beforehand.

TUESDAY 23RD APRIL 1996

Three days after promotion, Swindon beat Chesterfield 3-1 at Saltergate to secure the Division Two title. Steve Cowe's long-range opener was quickly cancelled out by Jamie Hewitt, but Peter Thorne immediately restored the Swindon lead. As time ticked on, a late Wayne Allison tap-in finished the job off right in front of the travelling supporters to get the champagne flowing in Derbyshire.

SATURDAY 24TH APRIL 1965

A gloomy phone call confirmed relegation from Division Two for Swindon and manager Bert Head. After a 2-1 defeat to Southampton on Saturday afternoon, Portsmouth know they will survive at Town's expense with just a draw in an evening game with Northampton. Pompey get the point they need, and Town discover their fate as they stop on the journey back to Wiltshire.

SATURDAY 24TH APRIL 1976

Swindon are awarded a hat-trick of penalties in their penultimate fixture of the season by referee Lester Shapter as they face Walsall at the County Ground. Trevor Anderson dealt with the pressure and the psychology perfectly. He scored them all, putting each in a different part of the goal. Dave Moss and Dave Syrett also scored past ex-Oxford keeper Mick Kearns. The comprehensive win also lifted Swindon out of the bottom four ahead of a final match with Wrexham.

SATURDAY 25TH APRIL 1914

Swindon claimed the Southern League title for the second time in club history, with a 0-0 draw against Cardiff City proving just enough to take the title. It needed some fine keeping from Len Skiller for Town to earn the point they needed in Wales. The celebrations couldn't begin until after the final whistle, when Swindon discovered Crystal Palace had also drawn, meaning the Robins just squeezed home on goal average.

SATURDAY 25TH APRIL 2009

Simon Cox scored twice on what proved to be his final appearance in Town colours at the County Ground. The goals secured a 2-1 win over Bristol Rovers which not only confirmed Swindon's League One survival but also took Cox to a personal milestone – 30 goals for the season. He's the first striker since Duncan Shearer to reach the landmark.

SATURDAY 26TH APRIL 1930

All-time top scorer Harry Morris put in a virtuoso display. He bagged all five Swindon goals in a 5-1 Division Three (South) victory against Norwich City at The Nest to take his tally for the season to 29.

SATURDAY 27TH APRIL 1957

Swindon, in their first season under Bert Head, showed some small signs of progress with big wins in their final two home games in Division Three (South). The last game at the County Ground was a 4-1 victory over Colchester United, with Andy Micklewright and Frank O'Mahoney grabbing braces. Head's side still finish 23rd and must apply again for re-election but history proves the first seeds are being sown.

MONDAY 27TH APRIL 1964

The first leg of the FA Youth Cup Final attracted 17,000 to the County Ground as Swindon's youngsters faced Manchester United. One of the classy wingers on display puts Town youth ahead – Don Rogers. The equaliser came from another winger who also went on to prove he could play a bit. His name was George Best.

SATURDAY 27TH APRIL 1991

Swindon made sure of another season in Division Two after a turbulent year, as Glenn Hoddle's side beat Leicester City 5-2 at the County Ground. Steve Foley does the damage, hitting a hat-trick in a frantic match which Swindon led 3-2 at half-time.

SATURDAY 28TH APRIL 1956

A 1-1 draw at Aldershot on the final day of the season ended a dismal campaign where Swindon finished bottom of Division Three (South) and are thus forced to apply for re-election to the Football League. Despite this, the board decided to continue with the policy of picking the team in consultation with the trainers, rather than appointing a manager to have full control of team affairs.

SATURDAY 28TH APRIL 1990

Steve Foley's second-half equaliser against Middlesbrough at the County Ground proves to be enough to confirm a place in the Division Two play-offs thanks to results elsewhere. It means they can relax briefly ahead of the final league game at Stoke City and that for the third time in four seasons, Swindon will be part of the post-season games to determine promotion.

THURSDAY 29TH APRIL 1976

Swindon's 2-2 draw with Wrexham at the County Ground was just enough to make sure Town avoid the dreaded drop into Division Four, with Dave Syrett scoring both goals in front of a crowd of just over 9,000. Swindon stayed up by just one point in the final reckoning, having been sweating on news from the other fixture involving two of the other relegation candidates, Sheffield Wednesday and Southend United.

SATURDAY 29TH APRIL 1995

Less than two years after celebrating promotion to the top flight, Swindon were contemplating trips to Stockport County, Wycombe Wanderers and Wrexham after relegation into Division Two. A 2-0 home defeat by Portsmouth confirmed Swindon's fate and left manager Steve McMahon "lower than a snake's belly". While league re-organisation meant that four sides went down rather than the usual three, it's still a spectacular fall from grace and a feat that no other side relegated from the Premiership has managed the following year.

SATURDAY 29TH APRIL 2006

Twenty years after Town were romping out of Division Four, Swindon completed the full circle. Swindon rolled up at Ashton Gate needing a win against Bristol City – and some help elsewhere – to try and take League One survival to the final game of the season. A former City man, Aaron Brown, put Swindon ahead, but Iffy Onuora's side can't hang on to their lead. Dave Cotterill netted to make it 1-1 and send Swindon down in perhaps the worst possible venue to be relegated.

SATURDAY 30TH APRIL 1960

Swindon lost 6-1 with nothing seemingly at stake in an end-of-season Division Three game at Port Vale. Jimmy Gauld, ironically, scored the consolation goal. Gauld would later be found to be part of a plan to fix the match. Gauld, a 'fixing' ringleader at different clubs, was released at the end of the season. When the matter came to court, Gauld got a four-year prison sentence. Another player, Jack Fountain, got 15 months, while prolific scorer David 'Bronco' Layne was sentenced to four months. A fourth player, Walter Bingley, was also implicated. All received life bans from football.

SATURDAY 30TH APRIL 1994

After a mock funeral procession from fans beforehand, Swindon won their first away game in the Premier League – in their final match on the road. QPR were the victims as Swindon enjoyed a double over the west London side. Shaun Taylor put Swindon ahead before Les Ferdinand equalised, but for once Swindon were not to be denied with Jan Age Fjortoft and Nicky Summberee goals completing a 3-1 win.

SWINDON TOWN
On This Day

MAY

SATURDAY 1st MAY 1971

Swindon completed the 1970/71 season with a 1-1 draw at Luton Town, where Chris Jones scored a second-half goal to earn a point. The main talking point was what will happen over the summer after the board's purchase of Dave Mackay. It presumably meant the end of manager Fred Ford. Swindon finished the season in 12th place.

TUESDAY 1st MAY 1990

The police descend and arrest four key figures over allegations of tax fraud – another consequence of the illegal payments scandal. They are ex-manager Lou Macari, former chairman Brian Hillier, plus captain Colin Calderwood and Vince Farrar, who had worked on the club accounts. They are questioned at Bristol police station. Calderwood is quickly released without charge and able to focus on playing in the last game of the season, plus the play-offs (Swindon are already guaranteed a top-six finish). After questioning, Messrs Hillier, Macari and Farrar are all given bail. The trio would eventually face a trial at Winchester Crown Court.

FRIDAY 2nd MAY 1969

Swindon get the point they need at Rotherham United to complete a double of promotion from Division Three, to go with the League Cup. In a tense match at Millmoor, Swindon were trailing with a minute to go. Then Stan Harland, pushed up into midfield, Chris Jones with a through ball. The striker, on as a sub for Don Heath, calmly finished past Millers' keeper Jim Furnell and Town celebrated the greatest season, to date, in club history.

SATURDAY 2nd MAY 1970

There may not be another score-line like this in club history, as Swindon thump Italian giants Juventus in the Anglo-Italian Cup at the County Ground. The match finished Swindon 4 Juventus 0. Peter Noble opened the scoring with an hour gone, then came two strikes from Arthur Horsfield, before Stan Harland added number four in the 89th minute. For those thinking the Juventus team was light on quality, three of the starting eleven had been capped by Italy, while three more would go on to win full international honours later in their careers.

SATURDAY 2ND MAY 1981

A last-day 0-0 draw with Brentford at the County Ground was enough to keep Swindon in Division Three. Swindon actually finished in 17th place but were flattered by an incredibly tight bottom half of the table. Town ended up just one point above the drop zone. The point kept Swindon up at Sheffield United's expense.

TUESDAY 2ND MAY 2000

Jimmy Quinn was sacked as Swindon manager with relegation from Division One long since confirmed. The decision followed a takeover and a vote by the new board headed by property tycoon Terry Brady. Brady made the decision to bring in the vastly experienced Colin Todd as boss, with just one game of the season left.

WEDNESDAY 2ND MAY 2001

Bristol Rovers' defeat by Wycombe Wanderers was met with joy by Town fans, as it meant Rovers disappeared through the relegation trapdoor into Division Three, giving Swindon what had seemed an unlikely reprieve the week before. Swindon had given themselves some hope with Danny Invincibile's dramatic late winner versus Peterborough the previous Saturday. But it all seemed likely to go to the final day game at Stoke City.

SUNDAY 3RD MAY 1998

Swindon's season ended with a home defeat by Sunderland, with Steve McMahon's side beaten 2-1 as Kevin Phillips scored twice in the first half. Mark Walters netted a late consolation. The 14,868 crowd was infested with Sunderland fans, as they had hopes of automatic promotion, but they left disappointed as Middlesbrough clinched promotion instead.

SATURDAY 4TH MAY 1963

Maurice Owen played his final game in a Swindon shirt – setting a then club record 601st appearance. A prolific striker in his prime, Owen had dropped into defence by this stage of his career, using his heading ability at centre-half. Swindon drew 1-1 at home to Halifax thanks to a late Ernie Hunt penalty, with club captain Owen hoping to bow out by helping Swindon to a first-ever promotion.

THURSDAY 5TH MAY 1910

Swindon won the Dubonnet Cup by beating Barnsley 2-1 in front of 7,000 spectators in Paris. The competition for the FA Cup losing semi-finalists was held by a French sports enthusiast. Harold Fleming scored twice to mean Swindon had the pleasant challenge of getting a substantial bronze trophy back across the Channel.

SATURDAY 5TH MAY 1979

Swindon beat Gillingham 3-1 in an ultra-fiery Division Three contest between two promotion contenders. Terry Nicholl is red carded for the Kent side and Swindon went on to win 3-1 with two Alan Mayes goals and one from Andy Rowland. The previous meeting at the Priestfield had been full of antagonism, and after this match Ray McHale claimed he was 'targeted' by the Gills side for rough treatment. The bitterness lingers into the tunnel afterwards, with two of the Gillingham side, Ken Price and Dean White, subsequently arrested over an incident that sees Swindon trainer Wilf Tranter making a trip to hospital. The pair received a conditional discharge following a court hearing.

MONDAY 5TH MAY 1986

Swindon go into their final game of the season at home to Crewe Alexandra looking to reach 100 points. They sat tantalisingly on 99. A win would take them to 102, a league record. Town had to wait until the last 20 minutes to break the Alex down, when Peter Coyne scored. A crowd approaching 11,000 invaded the pitch prematurely, holding up the game for three minutes. Afterwards, Swindon got their hands on the Division Four trophy, the club's first-ever Football League championship.

SATURDAY 5TH MAY 2007

Swindon got the point they needed to earn immediate promotion out of League Two when they faced Walsall at the County Ground. Jerel Ifil's thumping near-post header from a corner put Swindon in front early in the second half. Paul Sturrock's side look on course to go up with a win, before Walsall's Dean Keates smacked in a spectacular free kick. No-one minds too much – Swindon still clinch promotion, while Keates' goal gives Walsall the League Two title at Hartlepool's expense.

WALSALL GOAL: JEREL IFIL SENDS SWINDON STRAIGHT BACK UP

SATURDAY 6TH MAY 1989

Swindon scored three second-half goals against Stoke City to confirm their place in the Division Two play-offs. Duncan Shearer netted just after the hour mark at the County Ground, then late goals from Tom Jones and Shearer completed a 3-0 win that guarantees a sixth-place finish.

SATURDAY 7TH MAY 1994

Swindon complete their first and only top-flight season with a 5-0 defeat by Leeds United, conceding exactly 100 league goals in the process over the 42-game season. Chris Fairclough's injury-time effort brings up the century past the hapless Paul Heald, one of many loan goalkeepers drafted in during the season.

SUNDAY 7TH MAY 2000

Colin Todd's first match in charge of Swindon is a 2-2 draw with Sheffield United in Swindon's final game in the second tier to date. Giuliano Grazioli scored twice after the Blades went ahead early, while young keeper Alan Flanagan is called into action after half an hour when Steve Mildenhall is injured. It would be his only outing in a Swindon shirt.

SATURDAY 8TH MAY 2004

Swindon and Hartlepool United met at the County Ground, with both sides knowing a point will be enough for them to make the play-offs. Swindon ease the tension by scoring early through Sammy Igoe, but Hartlepool's prolific Adam Boyd made things edgy by scoring with 20 minutes to go. Eventually, both sides settle for the point and it sets up Swindon for a two-legged semi-final with Brighton & Hove Albion.

SATURDAY 8TH MAY 2010

Swindon visit Millwall with an outside shot of automatic promotion. They have to win at the Den, and hope Leeds United can't beat Bristol Rovers at home. With Millwall also in with a shout of going up, it's a tall order. Danny Ward's early goal put Swindon in second place 'in running' for eleven minutes before the Lions equalise and go on to win the game 3-2. The result is ultimately academic as Leeds see off the Gas to clinch second.

SATURDAY 9TH MAY 1987

Swindon fans have great reason to enjoy a 1-1 end-of-season draw with Bristol City at Ashton Gate. With Swindon safe in the play-offs, Bristol City are looking for a win to join them. City striker Trevor Morgan put the home side in front with 19,201 in attendance. But Swindon kept plugging away and Peter Coyne equalised midway through the second half. The drama is far from over though, as City got a dubious-looking penalty when Joe Jordan and Tim Parkin tangled. The occasion proved too much for Gordon Owen though, and he rolled the spot kick wide of Fraser Digby's right-hand post. The match finished 1-1 and City blow their chance, with Dave Bamber knocked to the ground afterwards in a not entirely good-natured pitch invasion.

TUESDAY 10TH MAY 1977

Swindon beat Brighton & Hove Albion 2-1 in an end-of-season Division Three contest. It's a re-arranged game from New Year's Day, which referee Alan Robinson had controversially decided to call off in the second half with Swindon 4-0 up after he decided sleet had made an icy surface unplayable. Ray McHale, who scored in the original fixture, got his goal 'back' with a free kick. Dave Moss was the other Swindon scorer.

FRIDAY 11TH MAY 1906

Swindon striker Tommy Armstrong is born on this day in 1906. The Scottish forward is top scorer for Town in the 1933/34 season, netting 23 goals, 21 in Division Three (South).

FRIDAY 11TH MAY 1979

With promotion beckoning from Division Three, Swindon were beaten 2-1 at Sheffield Wednesday in their penultimate fixture of the season, with Alan Mayes getting the Town goal. Swindon went into the game in third place and even have title aspirations, as they are a point behind Watford and Swansea with a game in hand. The news is made worse with Swansea beating Chesterfield in their last game to move to the top of the league. Peter Shirtliff, a future Swindon assistant manager, proved to be one of the more solid obstacles in the Wednesday defence.

FRIDAY 12TH MAY 1978

Danny Williams' second spell in charge of the first team is over. Williams moved upstairs to a general manager's position – and the board began the search for his successor – having taken charge of more than 400 games in his two stints as boss.

SATURDAY 12TH MAY 1984

Swindon wrapped up their Division Four season with a 2-1 defeat at Bury in front of 1,214 fans at Gigg Lane. Eric Potts' late winner means Swindon finish 17th in Division Four, their lowest placing in the Football League since the end of the Division Three North/South divide. The board, though, go on to offer manager Ken Beamish another year in the hot seat, having given him a budget consisting mainly of dust and magic beans.

SUNDAY 13TH MAY 1990

Swindon take control of their Division Two play-off semi-final with Blackburn Rovers with a 2-1 win at Ewood Park in the first leg. Steve White gets things started. Then came a quite superb volley from Steve Foley from the edge of the area to make it 2-0. Rovers sub Andy Kennedy pulled one back to mean there will be some sweating to be done during the second leg.

TUESDAY 14TH MAY 1963

For the first time in Swindon history – promotion! Town needed a win against mid-table Shrewsbury Town at the County Ground to secure second place in Division Three, with a crowd of 20,273 crammed in waiting to see history made. It's a nervous Swindon performance, but finally one of Bert Head's crop of youngsters, Roger Smart, conjures up a goal with two minutes to go. It completed a patient building process by the Town manager, who inherited a team in the nether regions of Division Three (South) when he took charge. Head would tell the Swindon Advertiser: "I was never more relieved in my life than when Roger's goal went in. I have always been confident, right from the early stages, that our youth policy would see us into Division Two. We have had our ups and downs on the way though, naturally, but our faith has never wavered."

TUESDAY 15TH MAY 1979

Any lingering hopes of promotion from Division Three disappeared as Swindon lost 5-2 at Blackpool in their final fixture. It was a disappointing note for John Trollope's career to apparently end; with Trollope keen to focus on his work with the youth team after being hauled out of retirement.

WEDNESDAY 16TH MAY 1990

Swindon fans take inspiration from the 1978 World Cup for the second leg of the play-off semi-final with Blackburn Rovers. The players, and in particular Argentinian manager Ossie Ardiles, are greeted with a ticker-tape style reception as they make their way out on to the pitch. The reception had the desired effect as strikers Duncan Shearer and Steve White score in the first half. Swindon won 2-1 on the night, 4-2 on aggregate and earned a first trip to Wembley in 21 years.

SUNDAY 16TH MAY 1993

Swindon Town and Tranmere Rovers meet in the opening leg of the Division One play-offs. The game had an amazing start, with Rovers' defender Steve Vickers enduring a nightmare opening. He put through his own goal with a diving header, and then lost possession at a key moment to allow Dave Mitchell in to score. It's 2-0 before fans have had time to sit down. Craig Maskell made it 3-0 inside half an hour. Tranmere got a goal controversially disallowed before Johnny Morrissey pulled one back for Rovers. The first leg finished 3-1.

WEDNESDAY 17TH MAY 1978

Swindon appoint Port Vale boss Bobby Smith, 34, as their new manager. Smith had taken Bury up into Division Three but he'd just taken Vale the other way. Nonetheless, Town decide he was the right man for the job and agreed to pay Vale £10,000 in compensation.

SUNDAY 17TH MAY 1987

Swindon did enough to reach the Division Three play-off final. After their comeback 3-2 win at Wigan Athletic, a goalless draw against the Latics at the County Ground was enough to move into the final, where Swindon face Gillingham over two legs.

MONDAY 17TH MAY 2010

Swindon defied the odds to make it to the League One play-off final by beating Charlton Athletic on penalties. 2-1 to the good from the first leg, Swindon lost keeper David Lucas with a shoulder injury inside the opening minute and by half-time their first-leg advantage had gone when Simon Ferry miscued a clearance from a corner into his own net and David Mooney finished from the edge of the area. When Gordon Greer was sent off for a high foot midway through the second half, the tie appeared to be out of reach. The ten men equalised though after Danny Ward showed great alertness when the ball broke loose from Jon-Paul McGovern's miss-hit shot. Charlton defender Miguel Llera was then sent off for hauling back Charlie Austin, so extra time is ten versus ten. Charlton hit the post in the added 30 minutes but it went to penalties. The home side crack first in the shoot-out, with Nicky Bailey blazing wide. Town convert all five spot kicks – Stephen Darby with the decisive fifth – to go to Wembley.

TUESDAY 18TH MAY 1982

Swindon travelled to Newport County knowing they needed to win otherwise the club would be relegated to Division Four for the first time. Manager John Trollope called it: "The most important game in the club's history." Town hit the post when it's 0-0 with a Paul Rideout shot, but can't find a way past a County side who seem content to allow Swindon to play. Goalkeeper Mark Kendall proved a frustrating obstacle. When Roy Carter handled a cross inside the area inside the last ten minutes, Town's fate is sealed. Tommy Tynan scored the penalty and the club hit a new low. Trollope cited the departure of senior players and the inconsistency of some of the youngsters that replaced them.

MONDAY 19TH MAY 1980

After being at the heart of the Swindon midfield for four seasons, Town sold Ray McHale to First Division Brighton & Hove Albion for £100,000. McHale scored 42 times in his 216 Town appearances, with 14 of those coming from the penalty spot. He was a key part of the 1979/80 League Cup run.

WEDNESDAY 19TH MAY 1993

Swindon went through to meet Leicester City at Wembley in the Division One play-off final after a 3-2 defeat at Tranmere Rovers in the play-off second leg. In a game that ebbs and flows, Town are never pegged back on aggregate by a game Rovers side. John Moncur opened the scoring and that made it 4-1 overall, before Mark Proctor scored and Pat Nevin eventually finished after Fraser Digby can't hold on to a high ball. Craig Maskell finished at the second attempt. Kenny Irons' penalty rounds off a 3-2 victory for Rovers, but a 5-4 aggregate win. After the game, Swindon and Rovers fans swap scarves on the pitch in a good-natured finale.

THURSDAY 20TH MAY 1965

Swindon sack manager Bert Head following relegation from Division Two. It seems a harsh decision with the side affected by injuries to key players throughout the campaign, especially after his work in bringing through players from the club youth system and nearby non-league clubs, with Ernie Hunt, Bobby Woodruff, Don Rogers, John Trollope and Mike Summerbee just some of the talents he helped produce. Head is dismissed after 426 matches in charge.

THURSDAY 20TH MAY 2004

Swindon were knocked out of the Division Two play-off semi-finals on penalties. Swindon overturned a 1-0 first leg home deficit against Brighton & Hove Albion in the rain through Sam Parkin and Rory Fallon before Adam Virgo levelled the tie in the very last minute. Under the circumstances its little surprise that Swindon lost the subsequent shoot-out.

TUESDAY 21ST MAY 1963

Swindon lost 7-4 to an All Star XI in a testimonial game for manager Bert Head and Ron Morse. 11,000 turned up with Ivor Allchurch and Bobby Moore among the guest players for the visitors.

SUNDAY 21ST MAY 1989

An own goal from Jeff Hopkins was enough to give Town a 1-0 lead in their Division Two play-off semi-final with Crystal Palace as Swindon looked to climb from the bottom division to the top in just four seasons.

FRIDAY 22ND MAY 1987

Dave Smith's late goal for Gillingham means Swindon lose the first leg of the Division Three play-off final 1-0 despite having had the edge for most of the contest at the Priestfield Stadium.

MONDAY 22ND MAY 2006

Despite relegation into the Football League basement, Swindon were able to appoint Dennis Wise as manager. The former England international signed a three-year contract and he brought his former Chelsea colleague Gus Poyet with him as assistant. Wise promised a tough pre-season, saying: "I want a fit and strong side because once you have that you have a mentally strong side and that will help us no end." He also adds that he is not keen to play.

SATURDAY 23RD MAY 1970

Swindon won 1-0 at Napoli thanks to a Don Rogers goal in the Anglo-Italian Cup. The win puts Town into the final, and a rematch with the Neapolitans.

WEDNESDAY 24TH MAY 1989

Swindon can't hold on to their one-goal lead in the second leg of the Division Two play-offs. Town lost 2-0 to Crystal Palace, with their prolific striking partnership of Wright and Bright scoring first-half goals. It's no disgrace on reflection. Palace went on to win promotion and 12 months later were in the FA Cup Final.

MONDAY 25TH MAY 1987

Swindon recovered from a two-goal deficit against Gillingham in the Division Three play-offs. With Town 1-0 down at the County Ground, and 2-0 behind on aggregate, Peter Coyne scrambled a goal back, then the out-of-favour Charlie Henry arrived off the bench to volley in a peach of an equaliser. The rules meant a third game was now needed, with Selhurst Park chosen as a neutral venue.

WEDNESDAY 26TH MAY 1971

Swindon, the current Anglo-Italian Cup holders, drew 2-2 at the County Ground against Bologna, despite leading twice with goals from Peter Noble and Tony Gough.

MONDAY 27TH MAY 1940

The County Ground was commandeered by the War Office, with part of the stands to be used as an air-raid shelter if required. The club was effectively closed down completely during World War II, with part of the pitch used as a Prisoner of War Camp.

THURSDAY 28TH MAY 1970

Swindon won the first-ever Anglo-Italian Cup, beating Napoli 3-0 on the Italian side's home ground in a final marred by crowd trouble. Fred Ford's team produced a controlled and disciplined performance, with Peter Noble netting twice before Arthur Horsfield scored in the 63rd minute. A short time afterwards the home crowd turned on their side, beginning to hurl concrete blocks from broken benches on to the pitch, as well as bottles. Referee Paul Schiller decided the only safe thing to do is abandon the game with 11 minutes to go. Despite the anarchy in the stands, Swindon collected the trophy, and some of the home fans even applauded as manager Fred Ford ran to them, holding the cup aloft. Shortly after, the Swindon squad got off the pitch as the violence increased. The post-match banquet to celebrate was predictably cancelled.

MONDAY 28TH MAY 1990

A thoroughly deserved 1-0 win over Sunderland at Wembley (attendance 72,873) appeared to earn Swindon promotion to the First Division for the first time. Swindon dominated the game, with Alan McLoughlin scoring the only goal, a shot that takes a massive deflection via defender Gary Bennett. Several other chances come and go for Ossie Ardiles' side, with the normally reliable Steve White and Duncan Shearer unable to extend the lead. It completes an amazing rise from the bottom of the Football League to the top in five seasons. However, there is some degree of uncertainty overhanging the celebrations, as the club have yet to find out the punishment they will received for illegal payments.

SATURDAY 29TH MAY 1909

Harold Fleming scored his first international goal for England. The Swindon forward is on target as England win 4-2 against Hungary in Budapest. Fleming's is the third goal, arriving three minutes before the break.

FRIDAY 29TH MAY 1987

It's a second straight promotion for Swindon as they finally killed off Gillingham in the Division Three play-offs at Selhurst Park in a third game between the sides. Steve White scored the fastest Town goal of the season to put Swindon in front and his drive made it 2-0 in the second half, with Fraser Digby in fine form to thwart any prospect of a comeback. Around 10,000 fans celebrated at the final whistle.

SATURDAY 29TH MAY 2010

Swindon tasted defeat at Wembley for the first time, losing 1-0 to Millwall in the League One play-offs. Danny Wilson described the first half as his team's worst 45 minutes of the season. Town have one golden opportunity, when striker Charlie Austin takes advantage of a defensive mistake to sprint through. The ball bobbles wickedly on the new Wembley surface as Austin is poised to shoot and the chance goes begging.

WEDNESDAY 30TH MAY 2007

Swindon fans urge the club not to consider a groundsharing agreement with local rivals Bristol Rovers. Rovers have plans to re-develop their Memorial Stadium and need a temporary home while the work is done, but trouble in recent meetings sees supporters lobby strongly against the move.

MONDAY 31ST MAY 1993

Swindon beat Leicester City 4-3 in an epic play-off final at Wembley to reach the Premier League. Glenn Hoddle's side go 3-0 up at one stage, with the player-manager passing the ball into the net to put Town in front before the break. Craig Maskell fired in off the post to make it 2-0 from a tight angle then Shaun Taylor nodded in a third to make it 3-0 after 54 minutes. Leicester conjured up a wholehearted comeback, though. Three goals in 11 minutes from Julian Joachim, Steve Walsh and Steve Thompson pulled the game back to 3-3. At this point, both teams seemed to pause for breath. Then, inside the last 10 minutes, sub Steve White chases after a long ball and there's enough contact from Leicester keeper Kevin Poole to earn a penalty. Paul Bodin tucks it home and Town make the top flight at last.

SWINDON TOWN
On This Day

JUNE

TUESDAY 1st JUNE 1971

The Anglo-Italian Cup rumbled on and Town's hopes of a repeat final appearance were dealt a blow by a 3-1 defeat in Bologna in front of a crowd of 25,000. Peter Noble scored the only goal for Town. The format of the competition sees each team play four games, two at home and away. Twelve sides play in total, six from England and six from Italy, with the most successful English side to take on the best Italian team. Bologna, aided by that win, made the final.

SUNDAY 2nd JUNE 1963

Swindon forward Ernie Hunt added to his growing reputation by earning a first England under-23 cap. England were beaten 1-0 by Romania in Bucharest in front of 6,000 supporters with Hunt playing the full 90 minutes. Ernie Hunt, formally listed as 'Roger', his actual first name, had earned his call-up by scoring 27 goals in league and cup the previous season to help Swindon into Division Two. It made a change from one of his previous summer occupations – working as a barber.

TUESDAY 2nd JUNE 1964

Future England international and Swindon winger Mark Walters was born. Walters was signed in 1996 by Steve McMahon to add some extra quality to the Town squad heading back into the First Division. Walters would score 28 goals in 126 games, with some excellent free kicks among them. He would net 11 times in the 1998/99 season. However, Walters would show the traditional winger traits of quality and inconsistency. Later, his wages would prove difficult as the club's finances deteriorated and he was released, moving down the M4 to Bristol Rovers.

FRIDAY 3rd JUNE 1977

Swindon winger Trevor Anderson completed his involvement in the Home Internationals as Northern Ireland drew 1-1 with Wales. The Ulsterman had played in all three games of the annual series. The Irish finished last this time round and added defeats against England and Scotland. Anderson would win 12 caps during his time with Swindon, and play 22 times for Northern Ireland in total.

MONDAY 4TH JUNE 1973

Burnley spent £40,000 on signing Swindon midfielder Peter Noble after their promotion back into the First Division. Noble, one of the League Cup winners, was a Danny Williams signing, costing £8,000 five-and-a-half years prior – earning Swindon a healthy return on their investment. He would end his Swindon career with 80 goals in 256 games and twice be the club's top scorer in Division Two. Noble then went on to prove an effective signing for the Clarets in the top flight.

FRIDAY 4TH JUNE 1993

Just days after leading Swindon into the Premier League, manager Glenn Hoddle's departure to Chelsea was confirmed. It's a massive blow, with Town not only losing an astute boss, but arguably their most influential player. The day also goes on to contain one more unexpected twist. Everything appears to have been agreed, with Hoddle deciding to move on and John Gorman following him to Stamford Bridge. Swindon chairman Ray Hardman then calls Gorman back into the boardroom – and offers him the manager's job, seemingly out of the blue! Gorman, put on the spot, can't resist the chance of managing in the top flight and accepts the considerable task of becoming Hoddle's successor and trying to keep a newly-promoted club in the Premiership.

SATURDAY 5TH JUNE 1971

Peter Noble's 89th-minute goal gave Swindon a last-minute Anglo-Italian Cup win at Sampdoria, but it's not enough to put Town back in the final. Noble's winner follows an early Steve Peploe goal before a Luis Suarez penalty made it 1-1. Blackpool's superior goal difference with a record of two wins, a draw and a defeat was enough to send them through to the final.

TUESDAY 6TH JUNE 1995

Steve McMahon spent £100,000 on the Bolton centre-half Mark Seagraves following relegation into Division Two. Seagraves had played against Swindon in the League Cup semi-finals the previous season. Born in Bootle, Seagraves had been at Liverpool as a youngster but was released without playing a senior game. The defender was never a popular figure, and left after 79 games in three seasons, joining Barrow.

FRIDAY 7TH JUNE 1899

Swindon's first modern manager, Ted Vizard, was born on this day. Vizard was appointed in 1933 with secretary/boss Sam Allen, who had run the team, reaching his 60s. Vizard, a former Welsh international, would spend six years in the manager's hot seat. His time in charge was fairly hit and miss. There were some good and bad seasons in Division Three (South) plus a painful FA Cup exit against Southall. He also made the club's first £1,000 signing, striker Ben Morton. At the end of the last season before World War II, Vizard left to join Queens Park Rangers.

THURSDAY 7TH JUNE 1990

Swindon discovered their fate after a Football League hearing into illegal payments to players. Town have already pleaded guilty to more than 30 charges of wrongdoing. After an eight-hour hearing at Villa Park the Football League delivers its brutal verdict. The league concludes there were "serious and persistent" breaches of the rules, going back to 1985. David Dent, the Football League secretary, then announced that the club would be dumped down into the Third Division – having just won promotion to the First. The verdict left the club directors barely able to speak to the assembled media, with angry supporters gathering at the County Ground to vent their frustration.

TUESDAY 8TH JUNE 1965

Swindon name their new manager after the decision was taken to replace Bert Head. The board plump for a Yorkshire man, Danny Williams. Before moving to the County Ground, Williams had spent his entire career with Rotherham United playing more than 600 games before taking over as manager in 1962 – at this time the Millers were a solid mid-table Second Division outfit. Williams would be a great believer in allowing his players to express themselves and to try and attack and outscore their opponents. His initial task was to rebuild the side in Division Three with the departures of some of the youngsters that had done so well under Bert Head now inevitable. Williams would use his knowledge of the north to make some raids on Newcastle United while his upbeat personality would make a positive impact on players and fans alike.

WEDNESDAY 9TH JUNE 1999

Swindon sign a striker who helped bring about one of their worst results of the last 20 years, when they bring in Giuliano Grazioli from Peterborough United. He had been part of the Stevenage side that knocked Steve McMahon's side out of the FA Cup. Grazioli would spend three injury-hit seasons at the County Ground, scoring 18 goals in 88 games, but he would have one lasting memory of his time at the club – meeting his wife.

SATURDAY 10TH JUNE 1967

Future Swindon striker Keith Scott was born on this day in Westminster. Swindon paid £300,000 for Wycombe to the striker as they struggled in the Premier League. Scott, a big striker, would score the winner in Swindon's first Premier League win, against QPR. He was also slightly faster than he looked, having a running style that appeared to be wading through treacle. After 12 goals in 51 games, Steve McMahon sold him to Stoke City for the same price the club paid.

MONDAY 11TH JUNE 1990

Alan McLoughlin became the first player on Swindon Town's books to play at the World Cup. McLoughlin came off the bench for the last 25 minutes of the Republic of Ireland's group match with England in Cagliari. During that time, the Irish equalised to earn a 1-1 draw. They went on to be knocked out by hosts Italy in the last eight.

THURSDAY 12TH JUNE 2007

Swindon defender Jerel Ifil's hopes of playing for St Lucia were put on hold due to paperwork problems. Ifil qualifies for the Caribbean island through his father, but difficulties in getting his citizenship processed are slowing down plans for a weekend debut against Guatemala.

WEDNESDAY 13TH JUNE 1990

Swindon announced that they will take their case against demotion outside of the football authorities. The club planned to go to the High Court to get out an injunction against being dropped into Division Three by the Football League.

MONDAY 14TH JUNE 1943

Norman John Trollope was born on this day in Wroughton. One of twins, and the youngest of five children, Trollope would go on to be an enduring feature in the club's history for almost 40 years. As a player, he won promotion twice, showing considerable ability as an attacking full-back to go with exceptional loyalty. His 770 league appearances for one club remains a record that seems never likely to be matched and in total he played 889 games for the club, including the 1969 League Cup Final. Sadly, his spell as manager coincided with one of the most impoverished times in club history, and during his tenure the club suffered a first relegation to Division Four. He'd also worked behind the scenes as youth-team coach and as Lou Macari's assistant following Harry Gregg's departure.

SATURDAY 15TH JUNE 1985

Swindon bid farewell to forward Alan Mayes, who signed for Carlisle United on a free transfer. Mayes has spent two successful seasons at the County Ground having originally left in December 1980 to join Chelsea.

TUESDAY 16TH JUNE 1912

There's no off-season for Swindon's hardworking squad. They spend the summer on a tour of South America, playing against a whole variety of opponents. Today is the first match, a 2-2 draw with the Northern Argentina Select XI.

THURSDAY 17TH JUNE 2004

Swindon sign non-league striker Lloyd Opara from Grays Athletic. Opara plays just one game, a League Cup victory over Rushden & Diamonds, before deciding he can't settle with the club, and is released in September.

TUESDAY 18TH JUNE 1946

Irish striker Ray Treacy was born in Dublin on this day. Treacy, an Irish international, was signed from Charlton for a club record £35,000 in 1972 by Dave Mackay. He would score 18 goals in 61 games before being sold to Preston North End just over 18 months later.

SUNDAY 19TH JUNE 1994

Fresh from his spectacular end to the Premier League season, striker Jan Age Fjortoft played for Norway in the World Cup in their opening game. Fjortoft helps Egil Olsen's side beat Mexico 1-0. Norway's group ends with all four teams on four points, but Fjortoft has to head back home at the end of the group stages without a goal

MONDAY 20TH JUNE 1988

Striker Jimmy Quinn left Swindon to sign for Leicester City. A tribunal sets the fee for the Ulsterman at £210,000. Quinn had scored 31 goals the previous season – 21 in the league – as Swindon settled comfortably into Division Two. It completed his second spell at the club, having originally been signed from non-league Oswestry Town by John Trollope.

THURSDAY 21ST JUNE 1984

Club sponsor Lowndes Lambert make a significant offer to the board. They will put in a substantial sum of cash – on the condition a new, high profile, player manager is appointed. The board accept, and so the offer of a new contract to current boss Ken Beamish is withdrawn. Beamish ponders his future and the search for the man to take Swindon forward from their worst ever Football League finish begins.

THURSDAY 21ST JUNE 1990

After an initial High Court hearing, the club decided to drop the threat of legal action to contest relegation into Division Three, despite fans' efforts to raise funds. The matter will now be placed in the hands of a Football Association appeals panel – a matter that would go on to drive another wedge between the FA and the Football League.

TUESDAY 21ST JUNE 1994

Two of Swindon's best performers in the Premier League left the club. West Ham signed the player of the season, John Moncur, in a £1m deal, while Nicky Summerbee followed the route trodden by father Mike, leaving Swindon for Manchester City. The England B international headed to the north-west for a club-record sale of £1.5m.

WEDNESDAY 22ND JUNE 1988

After Jimmy Quinn's sale, Swindon spend a club-record fee on his replacement, handing Huddersfield Town £250,000 for striker Duncan Shearer. The Scotsman had been top scorer for the Yorkshire side, who had just finished bottom of Division Two by some margin. After a slow start, Shearer would go on to be a consistent, ruthless and prolific scorer. If it wasn't for injury in that first season, he would surely have gone on to score 100 goals for the club. As it was, Shearer ended up with 98 goals in 199 games before his controversial sale to Blackburn Rovers near the end of the 1991/92 season.

TUESDAY 23RD JUNE 1998

Centre-back Alan Reeves joined Swindon on a free transfer from Wimbledon. Reeves would go through an odd transformation from one of Steve McMahon's unloved Liverpudlian contingent, to end his career by acquiring a slightly bizarre cult status. He reached his low point in the 2002/03 season, with fans calling for him to be sent off and making it bluntly clear they preferred defender Adam Willis. In 2003 Reeves took a coaching role and by the end of his career there would be what sounded like booing ringing round the County Ground – it was actually a booming chant of "Reeeeeves". He rose to became assistant manager, but the end was nigh when he missed out on succeeding Andy King as manager, with Iffy Onuora chosen. Reeves had a broken leg at the time. He ended up playing 237 games for the club.

MONDAY 24TH JUNE 1985

Swindon made what proved to be one of the most cost-effective signings of all time, with Scottish defender Colin Calderwood joining the club from Mansfield Town. A tribunal said he's worth £27,500. He would immediately be installed as club captain and be an outstanding centre-half, proving reliable on the pitch and rarely succumbing to injury. He would take Swindon from the basement to the Premier League before leaving in the summer of 1993 to link back up with his former manager Ossie Ardiles at Spurs. By that time he was valued at £1.25m. Calderwood's 414 matches places him tenth in the all-time appearance list.

WEDNESDAY 24TH JUNE 1987

Swindon made two signings. Firstly, they paid Sheffield United £40,000 for midfielder Steve Foley who would prove to be a small man (at 5ft 7in) but a big success over the next five seasons. Also arriving was Chester midfielder John Kelly. He would play just eight games before leaving to join Oldham Athletic in November.

MONDAY 25TH JUNE 2001

Swindon manager Andy King believed he had uncovered a gem when he signed French striker Eric Sabin from Wasquehal, with King making comparisons to Thierry Henry. There was a certain resemblance in looks and pace, but sadly not in finishing. Sabin took until November of his opening season to score and he would net just nine goals in 81 games, though his speed would periodically earn him a penalty from defenders as he sprinted past them.

WEDNESDAY 26TH JUNE 1985

Lou Macari made a popular move by bringing 33-year-old winger David Moss back to the County Ground on a free transfer, seven years after he had been sold to Luton Town. Moss had been a big hit in the 1970s at the County Ground contributing plenty of crosses and goals from the right wing. In fact, he'd clocked up two 20-goal campaigns before his move to Kenilworth Road. Moss played with Steve White there, who spoke warmly of his abilities. His return would be short lived though, with Moss playing just five games before injury ended his professional career. He would go on to be a coach and have one chance at management in the Football League, with Macclesfield Town.

SUNDAY 27TH JUNE 1982

Centre-half Jerel Ifil was born on this day in Wembley. Ifil would become known as 'The Beast' during his time at the club, finally joining for £70,000 after a number of loan spells from Watford. Ifil, at his best, would be an aggressive man marker who could bully strikers out of a game. Occasionally, though, his mind would wander. Ifil's first league goal would the header in the game with Walsall that would confirm promotion from League Two before he left in 2009 to join Aberdeen.

FRIDAY 28TH JUNE 1985

Winger Garry Nelson left Swindon after two seasons – signing for Plymouth Argyle for £15,000. Nelson didn't particularly enjoy his time at the club and would be a much bigger hit for Brighton & Hove Albion. He would also gain fame for his two books about life as a 'journeyman' at Charlton and his time on the coaching staff at Torquay United. His thoughts on another ex-Swindon player, Jon Gittens, make for particularly interesting reading…

TUESDAY 28TH JUNE 1988

A summer of striker sales and signings continued apace. After the departure of Jimmy Quinn and the arrival of new boy Duncan Shearer, Dave Bamber was now on the move. He joined Watford for just over £100,000. Bamber scored 21 goals in Town's successful play-off season in Division Three in the 1986/87 season, following it up with 18 goals with Town in Division Two. His ability to win penalties should also not be underestimated.

SATURDAY 29TH JUNE 1912

Swindon remain unbeaten during their off-season South American tour. This time they see of a Rosario League XI 3-1. Archie Bown scored twice, with inside left Billy Batty getting the other.

FRIDAY 30TH JUNE 1978

'The Animal' arrives at the County Ground, with bearded left winger Brian Williams joining the Robins from QPR. Williams is reunited with his former manager Bobby Smith, who gave him his start at Bury. He would spend three seasons with Town, scoring 10 goals in 122 matches before he went down the M4 to Bristol Rovers as part of the deal that brought Gary Emmanuel to the club.

SATURDAY 30TH JUNE 2007

It's the deadline for Swindon to pay money owed to creditors as part of the Company Voluntary Arrangement for exiting administration. £900,000 needs to be found or the club face the possibility of a winding up order. The club insist that fans should not be worried as the clock ticks onwards.

SWINDON TOWN
On This Day

JULY

THURSDAY 1st JULY 1943

Swindon winger Eric Weaver is born on this day. Weaver was a typical Bert Head signing; he was spotted playing for non-league Trowbridge Town. He would have two spells with the club, becoming a regular in the 1965/66 season. Weaver's son, Jason, would be a successful sportsman – he grew up to be a classic-winning jockey who rode more than 1,000 winners.

MONDAY 2nd JULY 1990

After long deliberations at the Cumberland Hotel, the Football Association appeals panel delivers its verdict on Swindon's two-division demotion for financial irregularities. Passions remain high with a number of fans waiting outside to discover the verdict. The club had barristers representing them, as did the Football League, with the hearing taking around five hours. Eventually, there is a victory of sorts. The Town representatives have done enough to convince the FA that Swindon should stay in the Second Division, rather than drop into the Third. The committee say that the offences are serious, but feel the original punishment had too dramatic an effect on fans and other 'innocent parties'. Swindon had to pay the costs of the hearing, but the judgement made that a worthwhile expense. Sunderland, beaten so convincingly at Wembley, were ultimately given Swindon's place in Division One.

MONDAY 3rd JULY 1989

Lou Macari's reign as manager at Swindon is over. After five years in charge where the league position improved each season he resigned to become the new boss of West Ham United. Macari had long been seen as managerial hot property, with frequent rumours of moves to other clubs, having guided Swindon from the lower half of the Fourth Division to within touching distance of the First. Macari was in charge for 285 games, winning 138 – an exceptional success rate.

MONDAY 3rd JULY 2006

Defender Sean O'Hanlon, widely expected to sign a contract to stay at Swindon despite relegation, made an unexpected move to the MK Dons. The fee went to a tribunal, with a base fee of £75,000 plus payments for appearances and promotion. Swindon had the last laugh, as they were promoted at the MK Dons' expense.

MONDAY 4TH JULY 1988

Chris Kamara left Swindon to sign for Stoke City for £27,500, ending his second spell at the County Ground. He featured in 293 games and scored 32 goals, eleven of those coming in his first season of 1977/78. He was also part of the squads that won back-to-back promotions in 1986 and 1987. The ending to his career proved sour, in contrast to so much of what had gone on before. Kamara was fined by magistrates after running the length of pitch to hit Shrewsbury striker Jim Melrose – an action that saw him suspended by Lou Macari. He remains resolutely shy about just what prompted such an out of character occurrence.

FRIDAY 5TH JULY 1946

Striker Arthur Horsfield was born on this day in Newcastle-upon-Tyne. Horsfield trod the well worn path to Swindon from Newcastle when Danny Williams signed him in the summer of 1969 for £17,500. It was a club-record fee as Williams looked for some extra firepower for the return to Division Two. Horsfield scored 28 times in his first season, and particularly enjoyed the Anglo-Italian Cup. After more than 50 goals in three seasons, he was deemed surplus to requirements by Dave Mackay and was sold to Charlton Athletic.

MONDAY 6TH JULY 2009

Irish winger Alan O'Brien joined Swindon from Scottish side Hibernian. The former Irish international signed a two-year contract, but his first season is hamstrung by hamstring problems. O'Brien started just four league games, but he was fit enough to make substitute appearances in the play-off semi-finals, and final.

FRIDAY 7TH JULY 1871

Swindon goalkeeper and future club director Bob Menham was born on this day. He would be Swindon's keeper at the turn of the century, going on to play in 160 games. Menham would become famous, though, partly for a game he missed. He failed to catch the train for Swindon's Southern League match on December 28th 1901. There was no way to get a replacement to Kettering, so defender Paddy Fagan played in goal. The result was a 10-1 Swindon defeat. Menham was invited to join the directors after his career finished despite this considerable indiscretion.

SUNDAY 8TH JULY 1990

West Germany beat Argentina 1-0 in perhaps the least entertaining World Cup Final of the modern era. Maradona was left in tears after Andy Brehme's late penalty and Argentina finished the game with nine men. One of those who lasted the ninety minutes was Nestor Lorenzo. Ossie Ardiles brings his countryman to Swindon just four months later, signing him on loan from Italian club Bari before making the move permanent.

TUESDAY 8TH JULY 2003

Swindon manager Andy King was ecstatic after he picks up the striker top of his summer shopping list. Tommy Mooney signed for Town on a Bosman transfer from Birmingham. Mooney would be player of the season, scoring 20 goals and forming a destructive striking partnership with Sam Parkin. His Swindon career would end with a miss in a play-off penalty shoot-out. The club tried to extend his contract, but Mooney claimed they had not matched a promised offer earlier in the season. He ended up signing for Oxford United, a division below Swindon – and failing to recreate his success at the County Ground.

WEDNESDAY 8TH JULY 2009

After 32 goals in the previous season, top scorer Simon Cox was sold to West Bromwich Albion. Cox commanded an initial £1.5m fee which could rise to £1.9m based on appearances and other clauses. Chairman Andrew Fitton was happy with the deal, saying; "He did a great job for us and we did a great job for him. It represents fair value." Cox had also been linked with moves to Leicester City and Glasgow Celtic.

TUESDAY 9TH JULY 1912

Swindon completed their South American tour with another victory in Argentina. Bob Jefferson's goal earned a 1-0 win over the Argentinean-Born XI, which was thought to effectively be the national side. Swindon went through the tour unbeaten. Secretary-manager Sam Allen was impressed with some of the players they faced, but he believed that they "look on individual exploits as the main thing, and every time there was a chance to show clever work single-handed, it was taken".

MONDAY 10TH JULY 1944

Swindon striker Alan Fowler died in World War II. Fowler and the Dorsetshire regiment had not been part of the initial wave of troops landing on D-Day, but he was involved in some particularly savage fighting to try and liberate two towns in Normandy, Eterville and Martot. The towns, and the nearby area, were seen as of vital strategic importance in giving the Allies a foothold in northern France. All the more sadly, it appears as if Fowler died as a result of 'friendly fire' as part of an RAF bombing raid.

SUNDAY 11TH JULY 2004

Swindon sold young centre-back Leigh Mills to Tottenham Hotspur before he played a first-team game for the club after he had impressed at England under-16 and under-17 level. Mills left for an undisclosed fee, but would never feature for the Spurs first team. He would play eight games for Gillingham on loan, scoring once and at the time of writing he appears to have drifted out of the professional game.

SATURDAY 12TH JULY 2008

Swindon met one of Turkey's biggest clubs as they took on Fenerbahce as part of a pre-season trip to Austria. Fenerbahce included Serbian international striker Mateja Kezman and Brazil's legendary full-back Roberto Carlos in their side. Not only did Swindon get a 1-1 draw, but the equaliser by Simon Cox was something special. He flicked the ball past a defender 35 yards out, then let the ball drop before hitting a dipping half-volley over the goalkeeper.

THURSDAY 13TH JULY 2000

The funeral of all-time Swindon great Maurice Owen took place at the Church of St Michael and All Angels in Abingdon. Owen would make a then club-record 601 appearances, scoring 165 goals. He would then perform different roles behind the scenes, eventually becoming groundsman before leaving in 1984 with a pay-off of just £100. Several former Swindon players attended to pay tribute, including John Trollope and Ernie Hunt, who said: "I've had a lot of honours in the game but to play with Maurice Owen was my schoolboy dream and nothing has ever eclipsed it."

MONDAY 14TH JULY 1986

Lou Macari spent £52,500 on two players as Swindon prepared for life in Division Three. Defender Tim Parkin joined the club from Bristol Rovers, while Exeter midfielder Martin Ling cost £25,000. By October, Ling would disappear, seemingly never to return, after playing four games under Lou Macari and just not being able to adapt to the team's style. Parkin would be a successful partner for Colin Calderwood at the back for three-and-a-half seasons, winning promotion into Division Two before eventually joining Port Vale.

WEDNESDAY 15TH JULY 2009

Swindon scored a useful pre-season win in Austria as they beat the Romanian top-flight side Universitatea Craiova 1-0, with a goal from defender Lescinel Jean-Francois.

MONDAY 16TH JULY 2007

Swindon nip along to Hunt's Copse for a pre-season friendly with Swindon Supermarine. Manager Paul Sturrock played a different side in each half, with Swindon running out 6-2 winners against their non-league neighbours. There were two trialist strikers, Portuguese forward Guiema, who scored twice, and Spaniard Ibon Arrieta. Swindon's sporting director Rufus Brevett was also present.

THURSDAY 17TH JULY 1969

After the euphoria of the League Cup Final and promotion into Division Two, came the bad news. Manager Danny Williams was leaving. Williams couldn't resist a return to Yorkshire when he was offered the manager's job at Sheffield Wednesday, who were then in the First Division. The departure of Williams came as a shock to many after building such a successful side. The move back north failed to work out – with Wednesday relegated during Williams' time in charge.

SATURDAY 17TH JULY 2004

Swindon won the inaugural Jimmy Davis Memorial Cup by beating Davis' hometown club Redditch United 2-1 at The Valley Stadium. His one-time teammate Sam Parkin scored both the Swindon goals. The event raises more than £10,000 for the former Swindon striker's memorial fund, with the cash being donated to hospices and children's charities.

FRIDAY 18TH JULY 2008

Swindon were beaten 3-1 at home by free spending Premier League side Portsmouth in a pre-season friendly in front of 7,500 fans. Simon Cox opened the scoring with a penalty before a strong Pompey side, including Jermain Defoe, proved too much to handle.

WEDNESDAY 19TH JULY 1989

Swindon chose Argentinean World Cup winner Ossie Ardiles as their new manager after Lou Macari's departure to West Ham United. The board take a calculated risk in appointing another player-manager but it pays off in spades. Although Ardiles quickly decided his playing days were over (he made just two appearances), as a manager he proved to be a great success, creating an attractive, passing side who would use a diamond formation in midfield to great effect.

SUNDAY 20TH JULY 1969

The experienced Fred Ford succeeded Danny Williams as Swindon manager. The move was designed to bring some level of continuity to the County Ground, as Ford had worked as coach at Swindon before leaving to became boss of Bristol Rovers. Ford's coaching and methods were highly rated by the players, so the transition proved to be quick and smooth. Ford would stay in the job until November 1971, when Dave Mackay assumed control.

TUESDAY 20TH JULY 1993

Dutch midfielder Luc Nijholt joined Swindon for the Premier League campaign, with Town paying Motherwell £175,000. Nijholt would be the midfield 'hardman' looking to break up play and was a regular over the next two seasons before returning to his native Holland. Nijholt had expressed an interest in managing Swindon whenever the post became vacant. At the time of writing he was helping coach the Qatar national side.

MONDAY 21st JULY 2003

Swindon's big pre-season tour began, with the players set to spend four days in Devon as they embarked on three games in a week. The first, on the Monday evening, saw a 6-1 win at Bideford with Sam Parkin scoring four times.

MONDAY 22ND JULY 1994

Swindon pay a club record £600,000 for the Newcastle United right-back Mark Robinson as John Gorman tried to bolster the club's defence. Robinson had suffered a broken leg while on Tyneside and had struggled to regain his place in the side. While not having a brilliant debut season, he was ever present in the Division Two title-winning side of 1996 and went on to play more than 300 games for the club before injuries forced him to retire in 2002. He also spent a spell as club captain.

THURSDAY 22ND JULY 2004

Hopes of building a new stadium on the Shaw Tip site suffered a fatal blow. Local councillors voted to keep a community forest on part of the area that the new ground would occupy. It meant the plan to move collapsed just three months after being announced by the board.

MONDAY 23RD JULY 1984

Having come close to appointing Phil Thompson, Swindon named 35-year-old Lou Macari as manager. It followed sponsors Lowndes Lambert's injection of cash into the club. Macari brought the experienced Harry Gregg, a survivor of the Munich air crash, with him as assistant. Macari knew he was taking on a tough task, saying: "It's the main part for any footballer to be fit. I will get as much enjoyment from seeing Swindon Town win a game as I did Manchester United." Macari immediately set down standards, holding individual meetings with every member of the squad to make his expectations clear.

MONDAY 24TH JULY 2006

It's revealed that midfielder Aaron Brown wants to stay with the club having handed in a transfer request. Brown was booed by fans in a pre-season friendly, having come back to the County Ground after an unsuccessful trial spell with Doncaster Rovers.

TUESDAY 25TH JULY 1995

Swindon paid £475,000 to Bristol City for striker Wayne Allison. The move was initially greeted with mixed views, but Allison, a genial figure, went on to do an excellent job in Town's promotion-winning side.

THURSDAY 26TH JULY 1979

Swindon centre-half Steve Aizlewood joined Portsmouth for £45,000. Aizlewood was at the club for just over three seasons, chipping in with 12 goals and on his day, being a more than capable player with the ball at his feet.

FRIDAY 26TH JULY 1991

Swindon paid £200,000 for Exeter's wholehearted captain Shaun Taylor. Taylor would be phenomenal in the 1992/93 promotion-winning campaign, scoring 13 goals – many of them headers from corners where he would beat his marker through sheer willpower. Taylor would earn three Player of the Season awards before he was sold early in the 1996/97 season by Steve McMahon to Bristol City for just £50,000.

TUESDAY 27TH JULY 1993

Swindon lost another player before the start of the Premier League season – striker Dave Mitchell. The Australian international was able to use a clause in his contract to move overseas for a fee of just £20,000. He signed for the Turkish club Altay Izmir. Mitchell had scored 16 goals the previous season, with his deceptive pace and hard work making him a good foil for Craig Maskell up front.

WEDNESDAY 27TH JULY 2005

Manager Andy King expressed his frustration at not being able to play any home friendlies so far in pre-season. The County Ground pitch hadn't been used after an Elton John concert held on the playing surface in June, and King was finding it hard to get a weekend opponent of sufficient quality after playing non-league sides.

MONDAY 28TH JULY 1980

Swindon opted for a trip to Scotland in pre-season to build up for the upcoming Division Three campaign. Today saw the second of three matches in five days, with Swindon winning 2-1 at Clydebank with goals from Andy Rowland and Roy Greenwood. Hopes are high for a good season, with the arrival of Nottingham Forest full-back Colin Barrett and Andy Rollings during the summer – and Town finish the tour unbeaten.

FRIDAY 29TH JULY 1966

Manager Danny Williams went to great lengths to make sure he signed centre-back Stan Harland from Carlisle United. Williams and chief scout Jack Colney camped outside Carlisle's Brunton Park overnight to make sure they got their man. Their evening of discomfort would be richly rewarded with Harland captaining the 1969 League Cup-winning side. Harland would be one of the victims of Dave Mackay's arrival, being sold to Birmingham City in 1971.

WEDNESDAY 29TH JULY 1992

The judgments are given in the tax fraud trial involving ex-chairman Brian Hillier, club accountant Vince Farrar and former manager Lou Macari. Macari was cleared of wrongdoing by the jury and he shed tears of relief at the verdict following a five-week hearing. Hillier and Farrar were both found guilty of what the judge calls "overwhelming evidence" of systematic payments to players that weren't declared to the Football League or Inland Revenue. The day after the guilty verdict, Hillier was given a 12-month prison sentence. Farrar, who worked part-time, was given a six-month suspended sentence.

THURSDAY 29TH JULY 1993

Swindon paid a club-record fee for a new striker for their inaugural Premier League campaign – Norwegian international Jan Age Fjortoft arrived from Rapid Vienna for £500,000. Fjortoft had been training with the side and had scored in a friendly with Finnish side FC Inter Turku, so hopes were high that he could make an immediate impact.

WEDNESDAY 30TH JULY 1969

Swindon rout a Gibraltar XI 8-0 in a pre-season friendly at the County Ground. New signing Arthur Horsfield netted a hat-trick, with the other goals coming from Chris Jones (2), Stan Harland and Peter Noble.

THURSDAY 31ST JULY 2008

With the start of the season fast approaching, and the club struggling to bring in new players, manager Maurice Malpas signed veteran French midfielder Lilian Nalis, who was not far short of his 37th birthday. Nalis was a free agent after being released by Plymouth Argyle.

SWINDON TOWN
On This Day

AUGUST

FRIDAY 1st AUGUST 1997

Swindon signed French trialist Philipe Cuervo after some impressive displays in pre-season convince Steve McMahon he's worth bringing on board. With Swindon having another Frenchman, Frederic Darras, on their books Cuervo at least had some Gallic company. Cuervo would show some real attacking flair during his three seasons at the club, but injuries never gave him a consistent chance to show his considerable ability.

WEDNESDAY 1st AUGUST 2001

Swindon confirmed manager Andy King had been sacked just days before the start of the new season. The decision to dismiss King came less than a fortnight after Danny Donegan had denied any plans for a change. There's speculation he already had someone in mind. Assistant manager Malcolm Crosby was retained for the time being, but reserve team coach Shaun Reid was also shown the door. Donegan has no qualms about the decision, saying: "We think we can bring new management into this club that will improve the situation and take us forward faster than Andy King." A group of fans gather outside to protest at his dismissal.

SATURDAY 1st AUGUST 2009

Paul Sturrock returned to the County Ground as manager of Plymouth Argyle for a pre-season friendly. Sturrock's Argyle beat Swindon 2-0 with a goal from Marcel Seip and an own goal from David Lucas.

SUNDAY 2nd AUGUST 1953

Future Swindon striker Peter Eastoe entered the world on this day in Dordon near Tamworth. Eastoe would be one of the few bright spots of Les Allen's time in charge. Allen brought the forward in on loan from Wolverhampton Wanderers and he would score on a semi-regular basis in a side doomed for relegation from Division Two. Danny Williams paid £80,000 to make the move permanent and the next season he would score 31 goals as Swindon came close to making an immediate return, with his movement in and around the penalty area his outstanding asset. In the end the talents of 'Thumbs Up', named for his individual running style, would make the top flight, with QPR paying £100,000 to take him to Loftus Road.

FRIDAY 3RD AUGUST 2001

Less than 72 hours after Andy King was dismissed, Swindon had a new management team in place. Former Liverpool boss Roy Evans was officially named as director of football and he brought in a big name, in all senses, as a player-coach, with Neil Ruddock arriving alongside him. Evans said he hoped to bring some stability to the club and that he was confident the team could make progress from narrowly avoiding relegation into Division Three. Evans was delighted to bring in Ruddock too, insisting his arrival was like bringing a Premier League player into the squad.

SATURDAY 4TH AUGUST 2001

Assistant manager Malcolm Crosby took charge of the team for a 3-0 friendly win at Dorchester Town, with the newly appointed Neil Ruddock among the interested spectators. Two defenders, Andy Gurney and Alan Reeves, scored along with Giuliano Grazioli.

SATURDAY 5TH AUGUST 2006

It's the earliest-ever start to a league season, and Swindon made it a memorable beginning back in League Two. New goalkeeper Peter Brezovan saves two penalties on his debut at Hartlepool – the first after just three minutes. Lee Peacock nicked a goal before Brezovan pulled off a second penalty save of the highest quality from Ritchie Humphreys. It enables Town to make a winning start under new manager Dennis Wise.

WEDNESDAY 6TH AUGUST 1997

Swindon paid £330,000 for Celtic striker Chris Hay. Initially, the signing would look like a steal, with Hay scoring 13 goals in 17 games, helping Town to a superb start to the season. After being ruled out by injury in November, Hay would score just once more before the season's end. He eventually was sold to Huddersfield for £75,000 in one of the club's periodic financial crises.

FRIDAY 7TH AUGUST 1936

Swindon sign experienced striker Jimmy Cookson, 31, from Plymouth Argyle. He did an excellent job, scoring 27 goals in 36 games to finish as top scorer, but Town had to settle for a mid-table finish in Division Three (South).

TUESDAY 7TH AUGUST 2007

Swindon drew 1-1 in a reserve team friendly at Hampton & Richmond. Trial goalkeeper Rais M'Bohli played but didn't look especially impressive and was not kept on. Less than three years later he was in goal against England in the World Cup finals. M'Bohli kept a clean sheet as England drew 0-0 with Algeria.

WEDNESDAY 8TH AUGUST 1984

New manager Lou Macari called in a favour from his old club as Manchester United visited the County Ground for a lucrative pre-season friendly. Swindon were beaten 4-1. Norman Whiteside scored twice for the visitors, with Swindon's goal a Garry Nelson penalty.

SATURDAY 8TH AUGUST 2009

Swindon were beaten 5-0 by Gillingham in a disastrous start to the League One campaign, with Simeon Jackson scoring a hat-trick. Manager Danny Wilson included four new signings in his line up. What chance can there be of a good season after that start?

SATURDAY 9TH AUGUST 2003

It's an awful start to the new season. Former loan striker Jimmy Davis died in the early hours of the morning in a car crash on the M40 ahead of his scheduled debut for Watford. Watford's game was postponed, with the reasons why not immediately made public but word leaks out as some of Davis' former teammates are in action against Sheffield Wednesday. Coincidence or not, Swindon are 3-0 down inside half an hour before losing 3-2. The result was an afterthought.

TUESDAY 10TH AUGUST 1993

With Swindon and Spurs unable to agree a fee for Colin Calderwood's move, a tribunal ruled on £1.25m. Spurs had offered less than £500,000.

SATURDAY 10TH AUGUST 2002

A new hero appeared to be born on the opening day of the season. Summer signing Sam Parkin hit a hat-trick on his debut, the third a late penalty, as Swindon beat Barnsley 3-1 at the County Ground. Parkin had cost £50,000 from Chelsea, but he had scored just five times the previous season when on loan at Northampton Town.

SATURDAY 11TH AUGUST 2001

Roy Evans' first match in charge of Swindon was a 0-0 draw at home to Peterborough United. Town got a point despite the sending off of striker Giuliano Grazioli against his old club with 28 minutes to go.

WEDNESDAY 12TH AUGUST 1981

One of Bobby Smith's expensive signings was shipped out, as midfielder Glenn Cockerill returned to Lincoln City after failing to shine at the County Ground. He was sold for £40,000, a loss of £70,000, after playing just 29 games in two seasons.

MONDAY 12TH AUGUST 1985

Swindon show a ruthless streak in beating non-league side AFC Bredon 13-1 in a friendly. Tony Evans and Colin Gordon both netted hat-tricks, with the other scorers Peter Coyne (2), Bryan Wade, Dave Hockaday, Dave Moss and Derek Hall. There was also an own goal to help out.

SATURDAY 12TH AUGUST 1995

After an indifferent start to the game, Swindon began life in Division Two with a win. Steve Finney glided in for a second-half winner on his club debut as Town won 1-0 at Hull City. With Fraser Digby injured, a young Irish loanee from Blackburn Rovers, Shay Given, played in goal.

SATURDAY 13TH AUGUST 1960

Swindon staged the annual pre-season match between the 'Reds' and the 'Blues' as the likely starting eleven took on the reserves at a match open to the public. The 'Blues' embarrass their supposed betters in some style, winning 7-2. When the 'Possibles' repeat the feat in a match behind closed doors, it left manager Bert Head pondering just who should be in his starting line-up for the league opener in one week's time.

TUESDAY 13TH AUGUST 1968

Swindon played their first match in this season's League Cup. Swindon beat another Division Three team, Torquay United, 2-1 with goals in the last half-hour from Roger Smart and Peter Noble in front of a healthy crowd of 14,702.

SATURDAY 13TH AUGUST 2005

After 17 unsuccessful tries going back to 1926, Swindon finally get a win over Nottingham Forest. Goals from Rory Fallon and Sean O'Hanlon earned Swindon a 2-1 home victory in League One. It's a welcome win after defeats in the opening two league fixtures.

SATURDAY 14TH AUGUST 1993

Swindon's first-ever game in the top division of English football ended in a 3-1 defeat at Sheffield United. John Moncur's quick free kick made it 1-1 and the game stayed that way until the Blades scored twice in the final quarter of an hour.

SUNDAY 14TH AUGUST 1994

It's the first game at the County Ground with the new Intel Stand on the Shrivenham Road side of the stadium. It replaces the old two tier construction dating from the 1930s. The top tier had already been closed down for safety reasons. Swindon beat Port Vale 2-0 in Division One in a televised game through a flashing Jan Age Fjortoft volley and a goal from Keith Scott.

SATURDAY 15TH AUGUST 1987

Swindon play their first game in Division Two for 13 years, with Lou Macari's promoted side beaten 2-0 by Bradford City at Valley Parade. Jon Gittens and John Kelly make their Swindon debuts.

SATURDAY 16TH AUGUST 1997

A 1-0 away win at Reading saw Swindon victorious in the last-ever competitive meeting between the sides at the Royals' increasingly dilapidated Elm Park home. Chris Hay scored inside the first 20 minutes in a game played in intense heat. It made it two wins in the opening two league fixtures after a win against Crewe Alexandra.

SATURDAY 17TH AUGUST 1968

Peter Noble came up with a late winner to give Swindon a 1-0 victory over Stockport County in their opening game of the new season in Division Three. Town haven't scored again on this day since.

TUESDAY 18TH AUGUST 1987

Swindon beat Bristol City 3-0 in the first leg of their League Cup tie, with a hat-trick from Jimmy Quinn. Gordon Owen's personal nightmare against Swindon continued. After missing a penalty against them on the last day of the previous season that could have put City in the play-offs, he was red carded with the score at 0-0.

THURSDAY 18TH AUGUST 1994

Swindon signed the former Oxford United winger Joey Beauchamp from West Ham United in a deal valued at £850,000 – centre-back Adrian Whitbread headed to Upton Park as part of the package. It meant his stay with the Hammers lasted just 58 days. Beauchamp, an Oxford fan, had been ridiculed for finding the daily commute from his Oxford home to east London too demanding. He wasn't keen on leaving his parents. Beauchamp would show very occasional flashes of talent – an excellent goal away at Millwall among them – but he was eventually shipped back to his spiritual home of the Manor Ground in October 1995, at a fairly handsome loss. It's where he would see out his professional career.

THURSDAY 19TH AUGUST 1965

Manager Danny Williams used his Yorkshire football knowledge to good effect by signing goalkeeper Peter Downsborough from Halifax Town. He cost £2,500 with midfielder Bill Atkins moving in part exchange. Downsborough would gain nationwide fame for his magnificent 1969 League Cup Final performance, and prove to be a consistent performer in 320 games, with his career at Swindon ending after a fall out with manager Les Allen.

WEDNESDAY 19TH AUGUST 1992

Swindon got a 4-3 win in a topsy-turvy derby game with Bristol Rovers, staged at Twerton Park. Glenn Hoddle's side sprinted into a 3-0 lead as Shaun Taylor finished a near-post corner, Dave Mitchell scored and Paul Bodin netted with a twice-taken penalty after a foul on Craig Maskell. David Mehew pulled one back but Swindon looked to be in complete control again when Dave Mitchell headed in his second after 47 minutes. But, Marcus Stewart gave Rovers hope and Paul Hardyman made it nervy with a late finish from a close-range free kick.

SATURDAY 20TH AUGUST 1960

Swindon manager Bert Head made the bold decision to give two 17-year-old full-backs their debuts in the first league game in Division Three. Terry Wollen and John Trollope both featured in a 1-1 draw with Halifax Town. It's considered to be the youngest full-back pairing in the history of the Football League.

FRIDAY 20TH AUGUST 1965

Winger Mike Summerbee left the club on the eve of the new season after relegation to Division Three. He'd scored 13 goals the previous season and had won England under-23 honours, as well as being part of the first-ever Swindon side to win promotion into the Second Division. Summerbee joined Division Two Manchester City for £31,000 and went on to become one of the club's most popular players, as well as earning eight full caps for England. Summerbee experienced all aspects of life while with Swindon. During his time at the County Ground one of his summer jobs was as a gravedigger.

FRIDAY 20TH AUGUST 1993

After two Premier League defeats and one goal, Swindon added a new striker to the squad, spending £250,000 on Wolves forward Andy Mutch. He had been an excellent foil for Steve Bull during his time at Molineux. Mutch made his debut two days later, at home to Liverpool.

SATURDAY 21ST AUGUST 1965

Swindon met neighbours Oxford United for the first time since their election into the Football League. More than 20,000 turn out for the 0-0 draw at the County Ground, which was Danny Williams' first match in charge as the new Division Three season got underway.

SATURDAY 21ST AUGUST 2004

On-loan striker Darius Henderson made a perfect debut. He scored both goals as Swindon beat Bristol City 2-1 at Ashton Gate. Henderson would score five times in six matches in his loan spell but the club was unable to persuade the player to sign on a permanent basis, despite agreeing a fee for his sale with Gillingham.

SATURDAY 22ND AUGUST 1953

Swindon make it two wins out of two under new manager Maurice Lindley by slaughtering Newport County 7-1 in Division Three (South) at the County Ground, with Maurice Owen getting a hat-trick. Lindley would not be a successful manager but he would go on to be Don Revie's right-hand man during Leeds United's glory years.

SATURDAY 22ND AUGUST 1964

Swindon suffered a disastrous opening-day defeat by Bury in Division Two that was typical of their season. After Bill Atkins scored in the very first minute of the new campaign, Bury equalised immediately and keeper Norman Oakley picked up a shoulder injury and was unable to continue. With substitutes yet to be permitted, full-back Owen Dawson went in goal. Swindon went on to lose 6-1, with Colin Bell predictably scoring a hat-trick.

TUESDAY 23RD AUGUST 1955

The greatest player in club history, Harold Fleming, died at the age of 68. Fleming rose from Southern League debutant to England international inside two years, with his playing career spanning Swindon's Southern League titles and entry into the Football League. All this came after he was spotted playing for a local side, St Marks.

SATURDAY 23RD AUGUST 1980

It's now three defeats in a row for Bobby Smith's side in the league, as they lost 4-3 to Fulham at the County Ground. Two of Smith's high profile signings, Andy Rollings and David Peach, both scored in a topsy-turvy game, where Swindon were 2-1 behind and pulled it back to 3-3 before conceding with 12 minutes to go.

SATURDAY 24TH AUGUST 1963

History was made as Swindon players and fans got a first taste of Division Two football. Scunthorpe United were the visitors to the County Ground, and 18,451 fans turned up to see Bert Head's side show little difficulty in adapting to the higher level. Two goals from Ernie Hunt and one from John Stevens made it a 3-0 win on the opening day of the season.

SATURDAY 24TH AUGUST 1968

Mr Reliable, John Trollope, played the last of 368 consecutive matches for the club. It had to be something serious to keep him from continuing – and it is. While jumping to make a defensive clearance, a Hartlepool defender landed on him in a heap and Trollope had his arm broken. Despite his arm going numb, he carried on playing – until trying to take a throw in. Only then was there a hint as to how serious the problem was. Trollope was taken to a nearby hospital, but local surgeons were unwilling to operate, saying it was a bad break. A plate was finally put in his arm midway through the following week.

WEDNESDAY 24TH AUGUST 1994

Swindon lost 2-0 at home to Atalanta in the Anglo-Italian Cup. The game was Steve White's 312th and last match in a Town shirt. White bid farewell with 13 minutes as a substitute before he joined Hereford United on a free transfer.

SATURDAY 25TH AUGUST 1945

With World War II over, football finally resumed for Swindon, with the County Ground knocked back into shape with remarkable speed having been acquisitioned by the War Office. Swindon were beaten 4-1 by Exeter City in the wartime league, but the result was far from the most important thing.

SATURDAY 25TH AUGUST 1984

Swindon player-manager Lou Macari made his first-team debut – and marked it with a goal and a win. Macari's first-half strike and a late effort from Alan Mayes helped Swindon to a 2-1 win over Wrexham after they had fallen behind.

SATURDAY 26TH AUGUST 1995

With injury problems leaving Swindon short of strikers, manager Steve McMahon gambled on playing defender Eddie Murray up front alongside Steve Finney in a match with Carlisle United at Brunton Park. The decision paid off handsomely as Murray thumped in a spectacular long-range shot from a tight angle to give Town a 1-0 won. It was to be his only goal for the club.

SATURDAY 27TH AUGUST 1938

The revamped County Ground was formally opened by Swindon MP Wavell Wakefield, a former England rugby international. A roof had been added to the Town End, at the cost of £4,300, raised by fans. The roof was then raised by Town fans, who enjoyed a 4-1 win over Notts County to start the new Division Three (South) season, with striker Ben Morton netting twice. Billy Lucas and Alan Fowler were the other scorers.

WEDNESDAY 27TH AUGUST 1969

After being denied entry into the Uefa Cup, Swindon took part in the newly created Anglo-Italian Cup Winners' Cup, travelling to AS Roma. Peter Noble equalised in the second half, but Swindon performed more than credibly going down 2-1 to the Serie A side… and there was the second leg to come.

SATURDAY 28TH AUGUST 1920

Swindon entered the Football League in the newly formed Third Division – and they've never matched their first-ever result. The opening game finished Swindon Town 9, Luton Town 1, and remains the club's biggest-ever Football League victory. Harold Fleming showed his class by scoring four times, while Billy Batty was the first league scorer. Batty netted twice, with the other goals coming from Bertie Davies, Bob Jefferson and Luton's Allan Mathieson putting through his own net.

SATURDAY 28TH AUGUST 1926

New striker Harry Morris made an immediate impression with a hat-trick on his debut, as Town opened the new season with a 5-1 win over Southend United. Morris cost £110 from Swansea City and already looked like a bargain. He certainly did by the time he left in 1933, having scored another 226 goals to go with his salvo against the Shrimpers.

TUESDAY 28TH AUGUST 1973

There are early indications that Swindon could struggle in Division Two as they are held to a draw by Division Four side Newport County at home in the first leg of their League Cup tie. Richard Legg, signed from non-league Chippenham Town, was among the scorers.

SATURDAY 29TH AUGUST 1970

Swindon beat Sunderland 2-0 in a game delayed when Sunderland's Bobby Kerr smacked into the frame of goal in front of the Stratton Bank, bringing it down in the process. The goals came from Arthur Horsfield and midfielder Tony Gough, in his only season with the club.

SATURDAY 30TH AUGUST 1969

Swindon gave notice that they will be a serious force in Division Two by beating Charlton Athletic 5-0, with all five goals coming in the second half. Peter Noble got a hat-trick, with John Smith and a Jack Burkett own goal all adding to the fun. The star was Don Rogers, though, who together with John Trollope wreaked mayhem down the Charlton right – or wherever he wished to go. It turned out to be the biggest win of the season for Fred Ford's side.

WEDNESDAY 30TH AUGUST 1978

Swindon scored an impressive win over West Ham United in the League Cup at Upton Park. The Hammers had just dropped into Division Two, but Ian Miller and Chris Guthrie gave Town a 2-1 win over a side including Frank Lampard, Billy Bonds, Alan Curbishley, Alan Devonshire and Bryan 'Pop' Robson.

THURSDAY 30TH AUGUST 2001

Swindon's League Cup-winning captain Stan Harland died suddenly from a heart attack at the age of 61. He'd been working at a supermarket in Somerset. He spent five seasons at the club, including that famous day at Wembley, before being sold to Birmingham City in November 1971.

FRIDAY 31ST AUGUST 2007

Manager Paul Sturrock made a triple signing as the transfer window shut. He brought in the MK Dons winger Jon-Paul McGovern who he knew from Sheffield Wednesday, plus striker Billy Paynter from Southend, who arrived in the pitch black before the window shut at midnight. While those two arrived on a permanent basis, Sturrock also took the Reading forward Simon Cox on loan. The trio were unable to play against Crewe Alexandra the following day, but all three to be influential players during their time in Wiltshire.

SWINDON TOWN
On This Day

SEPTEMBER

SATURDAY 1st SEPTEMBER 2001

Swindon player-coach Neil Ruddock finally made his debut, having become match fit, and found some appropriately-sized shorts. Ruddock marked the occasion by scoring a thumping left-footed free kick to give Town a 1-0 win over Colchester United. He celebrated by pointing to his name on the back of the shirt with his thumbs. He would go on to play 19 games, but things would deteriorate when Roy Evans left the club, and ended up in acrimony, with Ruddock planning to take the club to an industrial tribunal.

FRIDAY 1st SEPTEMBER 2006

Swindon made it six wins out of six to start the league season as Dennis Wise's side beat Chester City 2-0 at the Deva Stadium. Lee Peacock scored twice, both through set-pieces. The win matches a club-record start achieved in 1962/63 and was achieved despite the sending off of Jerel Ifil for two bookable offences.

SATURDAY 2nd SEPTEMBER 1939

Swindon drew 2-2 with Aldershot in Division Three (South), but most people's minds were elsewhere, with war against Germany imminent. This proved to be the last game of the season before the fixtures were cancelled for more pressing matters. The goals, poignantly, both came from Alan Fowler, who went on to join the army. He lost his life in the Allied invasion of Normandy.

MONDAY 2nd SEPTEMBER 1974

Manager Danny Williams decided the defence needed some bolstering as Town re-adjusted to life in Division Three, so he brought in the Norwich City centre-half Colin Prophett on loan. The two had worked together at Sheffield Wednesday. In his first start, Swindon lost 6-2 at Crystal Palace. He signed on a permanent basis at the end of the month. Prophett would prove to be a popular player over the next four seasons, not least because of his impressively large moustache and long hair.

TUESDAY 3rd SEPTEMBER 1991

Glenn Hoddle's Swindon side won 4-1 at Ipswich Town in an impressive performance in Division Two, with goals from Steve White, Colin Calderwood, Shaun Taylor and Micky Hazard.

MONDAY 4TH SEPTEMBER 1967

Swindon get an honourable 1-1 draw with Barrow in Division Three, after keeper Peter Downsborough has to go off when he picked up a shoulder injury in the tenth minute of the game. Joe Butler came on, with Stan Harland taking over as keeper. Harland was beaten on the hour mark by Bluebirds' striker Jimmy Mulholland, but Pat Terry popped up with a last-minute goal to give Swindon a very useful point.

WEDNESDAY 4TH SEPTEMBER 1968

Swindon were given a testing night in the League Cup second round against Fourth Division Bradford City at Valley Parade. Roger Smart's header from a Peter Noble cross put Swindon on their way, but it was a struggle after that with Don Rogers uncharacteristically quiet. The Bantams kept pressing in the second half and earned themselves a replay through a goal from Tony Leighton.

THURSDAY 4TH SEPTEMBER 2003

Swindon signed a future England international on loan when James Milner arrived from Leeds United. Although just 17 years old, Milner had already played for and scored for the Yorkshire side in the Premier League. Milner would impress on his debut against Brighton & Hove Albion in a 2-2 draw and score twice in six games, against Peterborough United and Luton Town, before heading back up north.

THURSDAY 5TH SEPTEMBER 1895

The first game was played at the County Ground site. Swindon beat Nat Whitaker's XI 4-1. The site of the pitch then was now where the cricket ground was situated. It would be another year before the deal was struck to build the original North Stand.

SATURDAY 5TH SEPTEMBER 1908

Swindon reached double figures, beating Norwich City 10-2 in their first home Southern League match of the season. For once Harold Fleming was outscored. While he hit a hat-trick, Jimmy Hogan scored four times. Archie Bown and Frank Heppinstall were the other scorers as Sam Allen's side went on to finish runners-up behind Northampton Town.

TUESDAY 5TH SEPTEMBER 1972

The reigning champions of England visited the County Ground, with Derby County in town for a League Cup second-round tie. A strong Rams side emerged with a 1-0 victory, thanks to a goal from Terry Hennessey.

THURSDAY 6TH SEPTEMBER 1951

Swindon swamped Watford 7-1 at Vicarage Road in a Division Three (South) fixture. Maurice Owen bagged a hat-trick, with two goals for Ulsterman Harry Lunn and one for Mick Betteridge and Roy Onslow.

SATURDAY 6TH SEPTEMBER 1986

Four years after being relegated into Division Four – after defeat at Newport's Somerton Park – Swindon made what proved to be their final visit to the somewhat ramshackle home of County. Town drew 2-2, with Bryan Wade twice putting Swindon ahead. Steve Berry got Newport's first equaliser, which might have prompted Lou Macari to sign him later in the season.

MONDAY 6TH SEPTEMBER 1993

Swindon looked to strengthen their Premier League defence with the signing of former England international Terry Fenwick, who Spurs were happy to let go at the age of 33. The combative Fenwick came off the bench that weekend to make his debut at West Ham United.

SATURDAY 7TH SEPTEMBER 1946

Swindon recorded a 7-0 victory over Aldershot in Division Three (South), which was the first of four wins in a row; the team scored 18 goals, getting five at Norwich, four at Brighton and two in a home win over Exeter, only to lose 5-0 to Cardiff two weeks later. Bill Stephens netted four.

SUNDAY 7TH SEPTEMBER 1997

Swindon played out an entertaining 0-0 draw with Nottingham Forest at the County Ground to take 11 points from their opening six fixtures in an encouraging start to the new Division One season. The game was put back 24 hours to avoid a clash with the funeral of Diana, Princess of Wales.

FRIDAY 8TH SEPTEMBER 1989

Striker Shaun Close celebrated his 23rd birthday by signing for Swindon from AFC Bournemouth. Close, by all accounts, would look frighteningly good in training but failed to translate that form into matches. He would be remembered as a forward who was the inverse of prolific, scoring twice in four seasons before being released and signing for Barnet.

SATURDAY 8TH SEPTEMBER 2001

Swindon drew 0-0 with AFC Bournemouth in a game marred by Keith O'Halloran's broken leg. O'Halloran was caught by Wade Elliott in a heavy challenge and left the ground on a stretcher. The game was played at Dorchester's Avenue Stadium while the Cherries' Dean Court home was being renovated. O'Halloran wouldn't play for the first team again, though he did spend two years trying to recover, making it as far as the reserves.

SATURDAY 9TH SEPTEMBER 2006

Paul Ince made his Swindon debut, at the age of 38, to become the oldest outfield debutant in club history. The former England international's arrival off the bench wasn't enough to save Dennis Wise's side from their first league defeat of the season, at Wrexham. Ince would play just three games before he was released, his signing becoming part of the boardroom politics prevalent at the time.

SUNDAY 9TH SEPTEMBER 2007

A new era appears imminent, with the BEST consortium seemingly poised to take over the club. Portuguese football agent Jose Veiga walked on to the pitch at half-time during the televised game with Yeovil Town to be announced as the new general manager, joining chairman designate Jim Little and sporting director Rufus Brevett in the new hierarchy. When questioned afterwards, manager Paul Sturrock admitted that he needed a meeting with the owners just to clarify who will be doing what. The new team in charge also say they are eager to develop the County Ground. Six weeks later the deal had collapsed with the club remaining in the hands of the Wills family and their associates, with both sides regarding the other as to blame. During this time, the players' September wages arrived late.

SATURDAY 10TH SEPTEMBER 1963

Swindon faced what might be their stiffest test yet in Division Two as relegated Manchester City visited the County Ground. More than 28,000 crammed into the County Ground to see City well beaten, as goals from Mike Summerbee, Ernie Hunt and Jack Smith gave Bert Head's side a 3-0 win to set a club record of six straight league wins to begin a season. Head's side have not only been victorious, but entertaining, scoring 17 goals in the process.

TUESDAY 10TH SEPTEMBER 1968

Swindon recover from going 2-0 down inside 20 minutes to beat Bradford City 4-3 in their League Cup second-round replay. John Smith pulled one goal back, before Don Heath was brought down and Don Rogers converted a penalty to make it 2-2 before half-time. Swindon start the second half strongly with a goal from Roger Smart, then Don Heath got his second assist, when Peter Noble headed in his cross. The Fourth Division side pulled a goal back with ten minutes to go but Town progressed to 4-3.

WEDNESDAY 10TH SEPTEMBER 1969

Swindon faced Roma in the second leg of the newly inaugurated Anglo Italian League Cup Winners Cup, trailing 2-1 from the first leg. The Italians attempted to keep the game tight in the catenaccio style that was prevalent, but they cracked inside the first ten minutes when Arthur Horsfield converted a John Smith cross. Horsfield was on target again with 20 minutes to go, this time taking advantage of good play from Peter Noble. A Don Rogers run and shot made it 3-0 and with the Italians dispirited, Horsfield completed a hat-trick when Rogers set him up with a perfect through ball. It finished Swindon 4 AS Roma 0 and was an interesting encounter for the English game by Roma midfielder... Fabio Capello.

SATURDAY 10TH SEPTEMBER 1983

In an indication that football was at a low ebb, just 1,091 were at Feethams to see Swindon lose 1-0 at Darlington in a Division Four contest. The defeat meant Swindon had picked up just three points from their opening four matches of the season.

SATURDAY 11TH SEPTEMBER 1909

Swindon beat local rivals Reading 9-1 in the Southern League – and they do it without Harold Fleming on the score-sheet. Freddy Wheatcroft scored four times, with Alex McCulloch netting twice.

SATURDAY 11TH SEPTEMBER 1976

Manager Danny Williams can enjoy a rout of the club who sacked him, as Swindon beat Sheffield Wednesday 5-2 in a Division Three game at the County Ground. Striker Dave Syrett led the way, scoring twice.

TUESDAY 11TH SEPTEMBER 1984

Swindon held a testimonial for long-serving manager Danny Williams and his assistant Jack Conley. The Swindon guest team, which included John Hollins, Chris Kamara, Alan Hudson and a certain Lou Macari, took on Southampton.

TUESDAY 11TH SEPTEMBER 2001

The night's League Cup games were played, although everyone's mind was on the attack on the World Trade Center in New York during the day. For the record Swindon were beaten 2-0 by West Bromwich Albion in extra time at The Hawthorns, with 14,536 people turning out having watched the day's events unfold.

THURSDAY 12TH SEPTEMBER 1985

With Swindon making a poor start to the season – one win in the opening five matches – Lou Macari brought in some competition for goalkeeper Scott Endersby, by signing the experienced Kenny Allen from Torquay United. Manager Lou Macari kept faith with Endersby for the next game but Town were beaten again.

SATURDAY 13TH SEPTEMBER 1980

Swindon manager Bobby Smith made the shock decision to ask John Trollope to come out of retirement after an unexpectedly poor start to the season – Smith's side have begun the league season with five straight defeats. He replaced David Peach and Swindon got their first victory of the season, coming from a goal down to see off Rotherham United 2-1. While Trollope had occasionally played for the reserve team as part of his coaching duties, his recall came out of the blue.

THURSDAY 14TH SEPTEMBER 1944

Swindon player Jim Olney was killed on the World War II battlefields. Olney, who joined the Coldstream Guards, died in Belgium, at the age of just 30. Olney had signed for the club in 1938 from Birmingham City. Lance-Sergeant Olney was buried in the Geel War Cemetery, around 30 miles from Antwerp, alongside 400 of his colleagues.

SATURDAY 14TH SEPTEMBER 1946

Twins Alf and Bill Stephens had a day to savour as Swindon won 4-1 at Brighton & Hove Albion's Goldstone Ground in Division Three. Striker Bill, and inside-right Alf, both scored in the victory. Both players had been signed from Leeds United in the summer. Alf would sign for Brighton next season, while Bill also made a move to the south coast, joining Bournemouth.

TUESDAY 15TH SEPTEMBER 1959

Swindon fielded their youngest player to date, when 16-year-old striker Ernie Hunt started in a 3-0 defeat to Grimsby Town in Division Three. The youngster had yet to sign professional forms but his selection was an early indication that manager Bert Head would have no qualms about playing youngsters who he thinks can make an impact.

TUESDAY 16TH SEPTEMBER 1980

The return of John Trollope helped Swindon continue their revival in Division Three. Trollope was part of a defence that kept a clean sheet in a 1-0 local derby win over Oxford United. Ian Miller scored the only goal, early in the second half.

SATURDAY 16TH SEPTEMBER 1995

Swindon completed a superb week in Division Two. After beating Bradford City 4-1 in midweek, Steve McMahon's side headed to Twerton Park for a local derby with Bristol Rovers – and repeated the feat. Kevin Horlock was the star of the show, scoring a hat-trick. It included a goal with his right foot, one with his favoured left, and a header. Rovers had got it back to 1-1 at the break, before Horlock's goals and one from Shaun Taylor saw Swindon run out comprehensive winners.

WEDNESDAY 17TH SEPTEMBER 1958

Rochdale made their first-ever visit to the County Ground in a Division Three contest and left defeated. Swindon came through 2-1 with goals from Peter Chamberlain, his first for the club, and Alan Moore.

TUESDAY 17TH SEPTEMBER 1985

Dave Moss played his final game for Swindon, as Lou Macari's side continued their poor start to the 1985/86 season with a 2-0 defeat at Crewe Alexandra. He scored 82 times in 275 games, but was ruled out for the rest of the season through injury. Moss was best remembered as a free-scoring winger in the 1970s before leaving to join Luton Town. Crewe's two scorers, David Platt and Geoff Thomas, both went on to become England internationals.

SATURDAY 18TH SEPTEMBER 1926

Swindon shared out 12 goals with Brighton & Hove Albion in their Division Three (South) encounter. The trouble was Brighton had the lion's share, winning 9-3 in the highest-scoring league game in club history. Swindon kept faith with goalkeeper Jack Bourne, despite the fact this was the new signing's debut.

WEDNESDAY 18TH SEPTEMBER 1968

Goalkeeper Peter Downsborough was beaten for the first time in Division Three this season as Swindon lost 2-0 to Bournemouth & Boscombe at Dean Court. Downsborough had gone 568 minutes without conceding before he was beaten by Ray Bumstead. Former Swindon striker Keith East's injury-time goal wrapped up victory for the Cherries.

SATURDAY 18TH SEPTEMBER 1993

Swindon produced a tidy comeback to earn a point against Newcastle United in the Premier League. Having gone 2-0 down, and with Paul Bodin missing a penalty, Swindon stormed back with two goals within a minute – first a low drive from Martin Ling, then a header from Andy Mutch, his first goal for the club since signing from Wolves. Mutch celebrated with a cartwheel as he took off towards the Shrivenham Road stand. Mutch's acrobatics were used regularly in the BBC credits for *Football Focus* and *Match of the Day*.

SATURDAY 19TH SEPTEMBER 1964

Swindon were heavily beaten by Portsmouth as Town continued to struggle in their second season in Division Two – Bert Head's side lost 5-0 at Fratton Park having gone 4-0 down inside 35 minutes. It's a third straight defeat – with no goals scored and ten conceded – after losses against Manchester City and Swansea Town. At the end of the season Swindon were relegated by Portsmouth on the final day; who finished just one point above them, with a worse goal average.

SATURDAY 19TH SEPTEMBER 1998

Fans discontent with Steve McMahon reached mutinous levels. Despite taking the lead against Watford, through a George Ndah goal, Swindon were 4-1 down with an hour gone of the match at the County Ground. At the end of the game a group of supporters said enough was enough and staged a sit-in. Occupying the centre circle they demanded the departure of McMahon and Rikki Hunt, the chairman who had given him prolonged and consistent backing.

WEDNESDAY 20TH SEPTEMBER 1978

Bobby Smith spent the healthy sum of £85,000 on a striker and gets richly rewarded when Andy Rowland agreed to team up with his old manager from Bury. Rowland goes on to net 98 goals and be a key part of the side who would reach the semi-finals of the League Cup. In the final stages of his playing career, he dropped back into defence before retiring at the end of the 1985/86 season. He would move on to the backroom staff and reach the position of assistant manager, before being dismissed in one of the many revamps in the Steve McMahon era.

SATURDAY 20TH SEPTEMBER 1988

After three draws and a defeat, Swindon got off the mark for the season with a 3-1 Second Division victory over AFC Bournemouth at the County Ground. Colin Calderwood and a Ross MacLaren penalty put Swindon 2-0 up, before Kevin Bond made it 2-1. Swindon didn't seal the win until Bobby Barnes scored with a minute to go.

SATURDAY 21st SEPTEMBER 1895

Swindon won 2-1 away to the Royal Ordnance Factories in the Southern League, with both goals coming from versatile Scottish player Jimmy Munro. Munro's career was cut horribly short when he died in 1899 at the age of just 28, having contracted meningitis. It was initially thought he was just suffering from a cold.

WEDNESDAY 21st SEPTEMBER 1977

Danish defender Kim Heiselberg was born on this day. Heiselberg would symbolise Colin Todd's brief stay as manager as a hurriedly signed overseas import of questionable ability. Heiselberg would play just twice, firstly in a League Cup match with Exeter City. His one league appearance would last 45 minutes – he was taken off at half-time when Swindon were losing 2-1 at home to Walsall and was replaced by Sol Davis. It didn't get much better – Swindon went on to lose 4-1.

WEDNESDAY 21st SEPTEMBER 1994

Swindon's League Cup campaign for the season looks to be over before it has begun after a 3-1 home defeat by Charlton Athletic in the first leg of their second round tie. Swindon old boy Garry Nelson scored twice for the London side to allow them to seize control of the tie. The home side's goal, which levelled things up, came from Keith Scott.

SATURDAY 22nd SEPTEMBER 1894

Swindon played their first match in the Southern League. The contest ended in defeat against neighbours Reading, with Town losing 4-3 at The Croft. The team included outside-right Robbie Reynolds, who scored twice, and the wonderfully named 'Babe' Andrews, who actually had the more mundane first name of Alf.

SATURDAY 22nd SEPTEMBER 1956

Swindon returned from Bournemouth on the end of a 7-0 beating in Division Three (South) despite the long-serving Sam Burton being in goal. The match finally seemed to bring the directors to their senses – who had attempted to pick the team by committee – with some help from player-coach Geoff Fox. A manager was appointed the following month.

TUESDAY 22ND SEPTEMBER 1987

Jimmy Quinn netted a League Cup hat-trick as Swindon upset First Division Portsmouth 3-1 in the first leg. Quinn scored twice inside the opening 15 minutes, then netted a late penalty with seven minutes to go, before another Quinn, Micky, scored to give Pompey some hope for the return leg. The Ulsterman also got a hat-trick in the previous round to help Swindon get past Bristol City.

SATURDAY 22ND SEPTEMBER 1990

Swindon made a brilliant recovery from going 2-0 down inside the first five minutes to beat Oxford United 4-2 in a local derby at the Manor Ground. Fitzroy Simpson pulled one back with a low shot from the edge of the area, with Steve Foley getting a close-range second before half-time. Ross McLaren's long pass was flicked on in the second half for Duncan Shearer to finish. Shearer would then make it 4-2 after Simpson's driving run into the penalty area – the win moved Swindon into fourth in the table.

SATURDAY 23RD SEPTEMBER 1961

Swindon finally got their first win of the season, at the tenth time of asking. Bert Head's side beat Northampton Town 2-1 at their old County Ground with goals from Ernie and Ralph Hunt, who scored with just 11 minutes to go. They are still in trouble though, at this stage, in Division Three.

WEDNESDAY 23RD SEPTEMBER 1998

After considerable fan pressure, Steve McMahon finally left the club as manager, having been in charge for more than 200 games. The departure was officially described as by 'mutual consent' but could possibly be considered more of merciful release for both parties. After taking the club down in his first season he did assemble a side that swept to the Division Two title, but fans would get tired of a pattern in subsequent seasons that would see his side tail off spectacularly in the final months of the season. Many of his signings failed to have the desired impact. McMahon's frequent changes of backroom staff saw many long-serving figures disappear, most notably John Trollope and Andy Rowland.

FRIDAY 24TH SEPTEMBER 1965

Swindon used a substitute for the first time in a Football League match when Owen Dawson was brought on to replace Ken Skeen in a 4-2 defeat at Southend United in Division Three.

TUESDAY 24TH SEPTEMBER 1968

Swindon moved into the fourth round of the League Cup with a 1-0 win over Second Division Blackburn Rovers at the County Ground. Don Rogers scored the only goal of the game with a run and shot to put Town ahead on 20 minutes. Defender Mick Blick, just 20, was drafted into defence with Frank Burrows ruled out and Swindon were able to restrict their higher league opponents to relatively few chances.

MONDAY 25TH SEPTEMBER 1911

As Southern League champions, Swindon were invited to take on Manchester United in the Charity Shield at Stamford Bridge. The Football League champions came out on top in a remarkable game, winning 8-4 with a double hat-trick from Harold Halse. Swindon had four different scorers, including Harold Fleming.

THURSDAY 25TH SEPTEMBER 1975

Up-and-coming Welsh referee Ron Jones was killed in a car accident. Jones was returning home after officiating in the Hereford United/ Swindon Town match in Division Three. The 37-year-old was due to referee in Europe for the first time four days later.

MONDAY 26TH SEPTEMBER 2005

Swindon decided to sack manager Andy King – for the second time – with the club in the League One relegation zone and fans voicing their displeasure at manager and board. Following demonstrations demanding King's head – and that of the board – he was smuggled out of a side entrance. King had to deal with a great deal of boardroom instability in his two spells in charge, while his interviews often produced eccentricities to delight or infuriate listeners in equal measure. The succession at least, was swift, as former player and now coach Iffy Onuora was asked to take charge, leapfrogging assistant manager Alan Reeves, who was recovering from a broken leg.

SATURDAY 27TH SEPTEMBER 1958

Swindon won 3-1 at Chesterfield in Division Three, with striker James Kelly, signed from Preston North End, scoring his second hat-trick for the club.

TUESDAY 27TH SEPTEMBER 1994

Swindon produced a superb turnaround at The Valley to overcome a 3-1 deficit in the League Cup second round. Striker Jan Age Fjortoft rattled in a 39-minute hat-trick to put Swindon ahead on aggregate before half-time, only for striker David Whyte to net with seven minutes to go. The unlikely figure of Joey Beauchamp came to the rescue during extra time, when his low, long-range shot cannoned off the post, hit keeper Andy Petterson on the back of the head, and went in. Swindon won 4-1 on the night and 5-4 on aggregate.

SATURDAY 27TH SEPTEMBER 1997

Swindon travelled to Manchester City in Division One, after an encouraging start to the season under Steve McMahon – it's just one defeat in their opening eight games. The optimism from that start was pretty brutally suppressed, with Town beaten 6-0 at Maine Road by one of McMahon's old clubs. Kevin Horlock, sold to City for £1.5m, was among the scorers. McMahon indicated his disgust with a triple substitution on 53 minutes, when the fourth goal went in.

WEDNESDAY 28TH SEPTEMBER 1960

An 89th-minute goal from David 'Bronco' Layne was the proverbial consolation as Swindon were beaten 2-1 at home by Watford in Division Three. It was just the striker's second goal of the season in seven appearances, having hit 20 goals the year before after arriving on a free transfer from Rotherham United.

TUESDAY 28TH SEPTEMBER 1999

Swindon, under Jimmy Quinn, pulled of a surprise 2-1 win over an expensively assembled Blackburn Rovers side in Division One. The Swindon side included Jimmy Glass in goal, James Williams at the back, and Frazer McHugh in midfield. An own goal from Simon Grayson, and an effort from Bobby Howe two minutes later, gave Town a lead they held on to.

SATURDAY 29TH SEPTEMBER 1934

Swindon continued with the trend of high-scoring matches against Brighton & Hove Albion. This time the two sides play out a 4-4 draw at the County Ground in Division Three (South). Outside-left Gordon Gunson scored twice for Swindon, while the Seagulls' wonderfully named Buster Brown bagged a hat-trick.

SATURDAY 29TH SEPTEMBER 1962

Swindon suffered a horrendous collapse to lose 4-3 at Halifax Town in Division Three. Town led 3-0 with 20 minutes to go thanks to goals from Cliff Jackson, Ernie Hunt and Jack Smith. Barry Tait then scored for Halifax. It's still 3-1, though, with ten minutes left. Then Tait scored again. With just three minutes left on the clock, Tait completed his hat-trick. The pain doesn't stop there, with Brian Redfearn scoring the winner for the Shaymen in stoppage time to complete the turnaround.

FRIDAY 30TH SEPTEMBER 1977

Friday night football was fun for Swindon fans as five different players score in the 5-0 victory over Shrewsbury Town in Division Three. Chris Kamara, Steve Aizlewood, Dave Moss, Chris Guthrie and even John Trollope were on target. It proved to be the biggest win of the season.

TUESDAY 30TH SEPTEMBER 1980

Bobby Smith was sacked as Swindon manager, despite the 1-0 win over Huddersfield the previous Saturday – he paid the price for starting the season with five straight defeats, despite three wins in the last four matches. The board decided that Smith's spending had backfired, with expensive arrivals like ex-Nottingham Forest defender Colin Barrett, Glenn Cockerill, Andy Rollings and David Peach failing to settle in successfully. Barrett played just five games; Rollings, signed from Division One Brighton & Hove Albion, only featured in a dozen league games. Cockerill was later sold back to Lincoln City at a loss, while Peach was dropped in favour of the retired John Trollope. Opinion was split as to whether or not the sacking was too hasty, with the upturn in form just before Smith was shown the door. Danny Williams, in his role as general manager, resumed control of team affairs while the board considered who to appoint next.

SWINDON TOWN
On This Day

OCTOBER

SATURDAY 1st OCTOBER 1955

Swindon took a hammering at Highfield Road against Coventry City, losing 6-0 in Division Three (South). Barry Hawkings was the star on the day, scoring three times, but there's no doubt who the most famous name was on either team sheet. Jimmy Hill was wearing the number 11 shirt for the Sky Blues.

TUESDAY 1st OCTOBER 1985

Colin Calderwood's late goal gave Swindon a much-needed win in Division Four, as Exeter City were beaten 2-1 at the County Ground. The victory ended a run of three straight defeats, with Town having only accumulated seven points in the opening eight matches. Colin Gordon's opening goal was the first in more than five hours of play, and although Martin Ling equalises for Exeter, Calderwood provides much cheer with his 89th-minute winner.

TUESDAY 1st OCTOBER 1991

Swindon put local rivals Oxford United out of the long-forgotten Zenith Data Systems Cup with a 4-3 win on penalties after a 3-3 draw in extra time. Dave Penney started the shoot-out and Fraser Digby saved his spot kick low to his right. David Kerslake missed though, before Oxford's Trevor Aylott was the man to crack, sending his penalty into a highly-delighted Shrivenham Road End. Glenn Hoddle and Duncan Shearer then have no trouble netting to earn Swindon a tie with Chelsea.

FRIDAY 2nd OCTOBER 1998

After dispensing with Steve McMahon, Swindon chairman Rikki Hunt chooses to appoint a successor who has a feel for the club, with ex-striker Jimmy Quinn coming back to manage the team that gave him his chance in league football. Quinn, alongside joint manager Mick Gooding, had taken Reading to the brink of the Premier League before being dismissed. Quinn quickly got an idea of the challenge he had taken over as he sees his side lose at home to Stockport the day after his appointment to fall into the Division One relegation zone. The unfortunate Ulsterman would see the financial situation of the club deteriorate throughout his time in charge, to the point where he would come out of retirement to don the red jersey.

FRIDAY 2ND OCTOBER 2009

Swindon decided to take a gamble on prolific non-league striker Charlie Austin, who had been scoring more than a goal a game for Poole Town in the Wessex League. He signed for a small fee, plus appearance-related money and a sell-on clause. By the end of the season, Austin had became an automatic selection, and despite not starting a game until the end of November, he ended the season with 20 goals after scoring in the play-off semi-final against Charlton Athletic.

SATURDAY 3RD OCTOBER 1953

Swindon recorded their biggest win over Bristol City to date, with a 5-0 derby-day victory in Division Three (South) in front of a crowd of 15,481. The goals were shared between Maurice Owen, Mike Bull, Jim Cross, Ken Lambert and Harry Lunn.

WEDNESDAY 3RD OCTOBER 1956

Bury's assistant manager Bert Head was the new boss of Swindon Town, ending a disastrous period where the board had controlled team affairs and left the side struggling grimly in Division Three (South). Head was thankfully given time to completely restructure the club's playing stuff, putting an emphasis on youth. His initial task was to make sure that Swindon didn't find themselves going cap in hand to the Football League in June to seek re-election.

TUESDAY 3RD OCTOBER 1961

Goalkeeper Sam Burton became the second man to play 500 games for Swindon Town. Burton kept a clean sheet to celebrate as Swindon drew 0-0 with Grimsby Town in Division Three. Burton was a big personality who enjoyed practical jokes and dressing room life. He reached his impressive haul of games despite not always being first choice – he was kept out of the side at times by Norman Uprichard and Ray Chandler.

SATURDAY 3RD OCTOBER 1964

Eight years to the day after Bert Head was appointed, Swindon beat Derby County 4-2 in Division Two, with one of the players Head had brought through, Ernie Hunt, scoring a hat-trick after Swindon had fallen a goal behind.

FRIDAY 3rd OCTOBER 2008

Striker Simon Cox saw his good work largely wasted in a 3-3 draw with Hartlepool United at Victoria Park in League One. Cox was set up twice by Billy Paynter to leave Swindon 2-0 in front at half-time, and he got his third with a superb individual run and finish. It was 3-0 Swindon after 52 minutes. After that things gradually disintegrated, with striker Joel Porter coming to the fore. Porter scored twice in the last ten minutes, with the second a bad mistake by keeper Phil Smith. Porter then scrambled the equaliser home in injury time.

SATURDAY 4th OCTOBER 1947

Swindon picked up their first win of the season in Division Three (South) after five draws and five defeats in their opening ten matches. It came away from the County Ground, as Swindon beat QPR 2-0 at Loftus Road. Young striker Maurice Owen got both goals.

TUESDAY 4th OCTOBER 1977

League Cup-winning goalkeeper Peter Downsborough returned to the County Ground for the final time as a player, with Bradford City. Perhaps not surprisingly, Swindon can't find a way past the 34-year-old as the Bantams win 1-0 in the Division Three contest.

WEDNESDAY 4th OCTOBER 1995

Joey Beauchamp's time at the County Ground came to an end when he moved back to hometown club Oxford United, initially on loan. Beauchamp had fallen out of favour with manager Steve McMahon – and the Swindon fans.

SATURDAY 5th OCTOBER 1974

Striker Peter Eastoe reached the ten-goals for the season mark. Eastoe netted twice in a 2-0 win over Southend United in Division Three at the County Ground. It's ten goals in just 13 games for Eastoe, who went on to net 31 times as Danny Williams' side finished six points off promotion straight back into Division Two – the team perhaps became over-reliant on his excellent finishing. Eastoe's career would eventually see him playing in Portuguese football long after his time at Swindon was over.

SATURDAY 5TH OCTOBER 1929

Swindon Town put Welsh side Merthyr Town to the sword in Division Three (South) with a 6-3 win at the County Ground. Petite inside-left Joe Eddleston scored a hat-trick, with Bertie Denyer and Fred Dent the other scorers.

SATURDAY 5TH OCTOBER 1991

Striker Duncan Shearer became the last player, to date, to score four goals in a match for Swindon. Shearer bagged all four in a 4-0 win at Plymouth Argyle in Division Two. The first was a diving header from a Micky Hazard centre. He drilled home the second from Nicky Summerbee's cross – Summerbee was playing at left wing-back on this occasion. The third came as he pounced on a mistake by the Argyle centre-back Adrian Burrows. The fourth arrived as he raced on to David Kerslake's long pass and nonchalantly rounded keeper Rhys Wilmot.

SATURDAY 6TH OCTOBER 1962

Swindon continued their free scoring form with a 3-1 defeat of Watford in Division Three, getting three goals in the last 20 minutes, through Arnold Darcy and Jack Smith (2). It's the fourth game in a row where Bert Head's side have scored three times.

TUESDAY 6TH OCTOBER 1970

Could another good run in the League Cup be on? Swindon beat Bill Shankly's Liverpool side 2-0 at the County Ground in the third round in front of a crowd of 23,992. Don Rogers scored twice in three second-half minutes and Liverpool can't find a way through the Town defence and past back-up keeper Roy Jones. The Liverpool side included Ray Clemence, Emlyn Hughes, Larry Lloyd and Steve Heighway.

SATURDAY 6TH OCTOBER 2007

Swindon savoured a 5-0 win over Gillingham in League One. Town went 2-0 up in six minutes through Jon-Paul McGovern's fine volley and Simon Cox's finish. Swindon toyed with their opponents in the second half, with two goals from Billy Paynter and a Cox second. It's a painful return for ex-boss Iffy Onuora, in temporary charge of the Gills.

TUESDAY 7th OCTOBER 1969

The fixture list was far from kind, handing Swindon a midweek trip to Carlisle United. Swindon returned from Brunton Park with a 2-2 draw in the Division Two fixture, with a goal from Arthur Horsfield and an own goal provided by Stan Ternent. The Town defence managed to keep perhaps the last multi sport professional, striker Chris Balderstone quiet. He spent his summers playing county cricket.

SATURDAY 7th OCTOBER 2006

Almost 47 years after their last visit, Swindon returned to Accrington Stanley for a league fixture. This time it's at the new Crown Ground, rather than the old Peel Park, which was now nothing but a field. Town came away with a 1-1 draw, and remained winless against Stanley. Lee Peacock scored a second half equaliser, when he finished off Fola Onibuje's parried shot.

SUNDAY 8th OCTOBER 1882

Future Scottish international defender Jock Walker was born on this day. Walker was signed from Rangers in the 1907 season and would prove to be a fine left-back who played an important part in Swindon's runs to the FA Cup semi-finals and Southern League triumphs. Walker would also earn international caps during his time with Swindon, playing in the home internationals. He was sold to Middlesbrough in 1913 after six successful seasons, for a handsome fee of £1,375.

TUESDAY 8th OCTOBER 1985

Swindon go into the second leg of their Rumbelows Cup tie with Sunderland trailing the Second Division side 3-2 on aggregate and it looked a long way back when Clive Walker scored late in the first half. Andy Rowland managed to get a goal back though, and Swindon have more than half an hour to find the goal that will secure extra time. The clock ticks beyond 90 minutes but up pops one-time bricklayer Bryan Wade – signed from non-league Trowbridge. He scored in injury time, then nine minutes later Wade netted the crucial third to put Lou Macari's side ahead on aggregate. It's the only time Swindon had been ahead in the tie, but the team hung on to score an impressive win and underline their improvement.

TUESDAY 9TH OCTOBER 1990

Swindon had to try and overcome a 3-0 deficit against Darlington in the League Cup – a side only just back in the Football League after winning the Conference. Fitzroy Simpson scored with a neat drive in the first half, then Shaun Close takes centre stage. The reserve striker hits the post with a shot that rebounds off defender Kevan Smith for an own goal. His volley was his first goal for the club in more than a year. Alan McLoughlin was able to round the keeper for the fourth in the second half – with the aggregate deficit now transformed.

SATURDAY 10TH OCTOBER 1964

Bert Head's Swindon side fail to hold on for a point against Coventry City in a Division Two game at Highfield Road. A goal from Ken Skeen and Ernie Hunt's penalty saw Town recover to go in 2-2 at the break having been 2-0 down inside 25 minutes. Ken Hale scored the winner with 11 minutes to go though and Town remained in trouble towards the foot of the table.

SATURDAY 10TH OCTOBER 2009

Swindon drew 1-1 in a fiery League One confrontation with Millwall at the County Ground. After Scott Cuthbert scored with a header from a corner, Jonathan Douglas was given a straight red card, only for the Lions to have Andrew Frampton sent off in the second half when his foot was high. A war of words flared up between Kevin Amankwaah and Neil Harris in the aftermath, with Danny Schofield getting an equaliser for the Lions.

SATURDAY 11TH OCTOBER 1969

It's one defeat in eight games for Swindon in Division Two, with the side clearly handling the step up well under Fred Ford. Peter Noble and Don Rogers were on target in a 2-1 win over a Sheffield United side who also have promotion aspirations. The game attracted an impressive crowd of 21,770 to the County Ground.

WEDNESDAY 11TH OCTOBER 1995

Former Spurs and West Ham United midfielder Paul Allen signed for Swindon on a free transfer from Southampton.

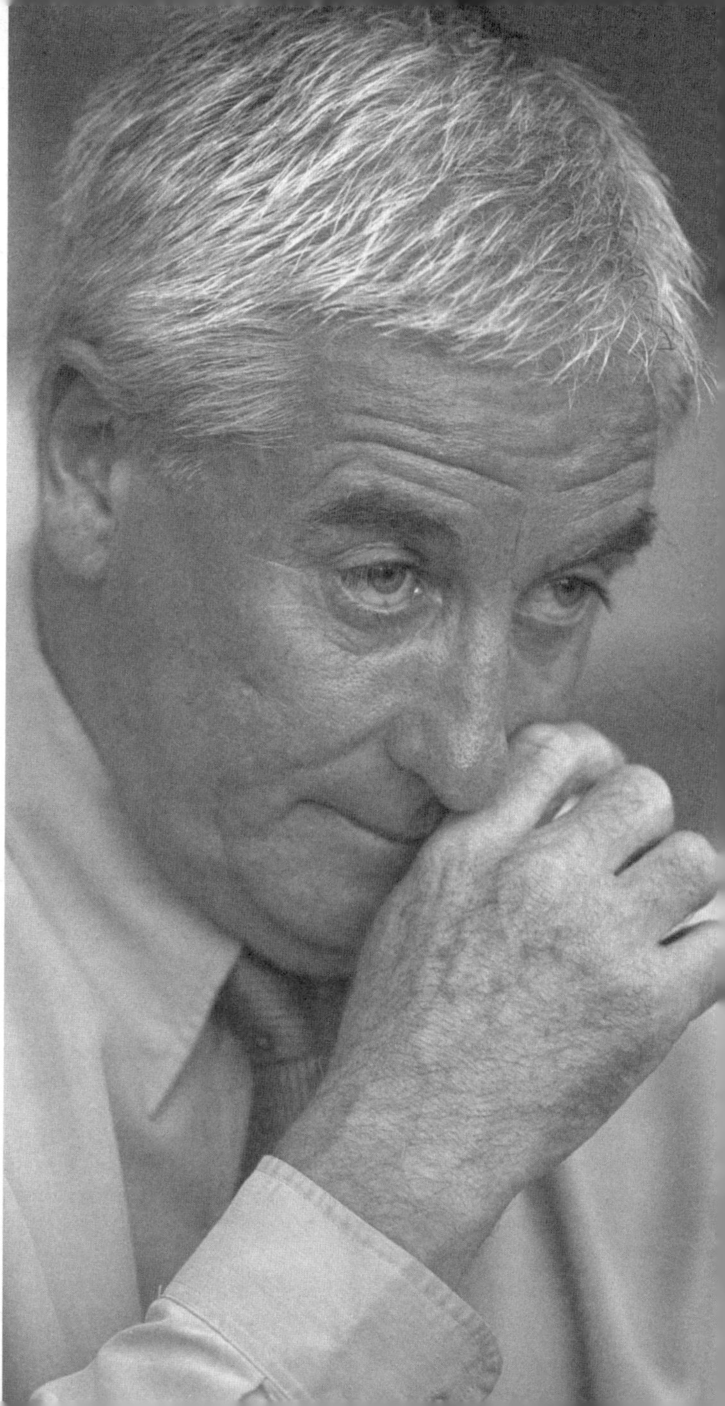

ROY EVANS: JUST A BRIEF STINT IN CHARGE

SATURDAY 12TH OCTOBER 1907

Youngster Harold Fleming impressed in the reserves having been spotted turning out for local side St Marks. Fleming scored twice in a 4-0 win over Salisbury and looked on course for a place in the first team. He was quickly given a contract to sign.

TUESDAY 12TH OCTOBER 1961

Swindon played their first-ever match in the newly created League Cup. It ended in a 1-1 draw with Shrewsbury Town in the first leg of the second-round game, thanks to a Cliff Jackson goal. The second leg also finished all square, and Swindon were finally knocked out in a replay.

SATURDAY 12TH OCTOBER 1996

Joey Beauchamp returned to the County Ground for the first time since leaving Oxford United. His harsh welcome from the fans was matched by that of his former team-mates. Beauchamp got some aggressive treatment from Mark Seagraves, Ian Culverhouse and Mark Walters. Referee Gurnham Singh took an intelligently relaxed view of some local derby challenges and did his best to allow the game to flow. After a Mark Walters header was tipped round the post, Kevin Horlock powered in the resulting corner for the only goal of the game, with Oxford missing some good chances late on to provide some very enjoyable derby-day fare.

SATURDAY 13TH OCTOBER 1979

Swindon made their first-ever trip to the rough and ready pleasures of Plough Lane to face Wimbledon in the Football League. They return having lost 2-0 to a brace from striker Alan Cork against the promoted Dons.

SATURDAY 13TH OCTOBER 2001

Roy Evans' Swindon side produce a more than useful performance to earn a 3-1 win at Reading's new Madejski Stadium in Division Two, with goals from Giuliano Grazioli, Danny Invincibile and a late clincher from Jo Kuffour, a striker on loan from Arsenal. The Royals defence included some familiar faces, in the Adrians Whitbread and Viveash. The victory kept Swindon in their highest position of the season so far, tenth place, above Reading.

SATURDAY 14TH OCTOBER 1967

Pat Terry scored a hat-trick within ten minutes of kick-off as Swindon sweep aside Bournemouth & Boscombe 4-0 in Division Three. Terry's goals came in the second, ninth and tenth minutes. He eases off after that, with Don Rogers scoring a second-half goal to complete the victory.

THURSDAY 14TH OCTOBER 2004

Andy King ended his search for a striker by bringing in Christian Roberts from neighbours Bristol City in a £50,000 deal. The pacy Welshman would find himself sometimes put out in a wide right position, but that would prove to be the least of his concerns, as he would later check in to the Sporting Chance clinic, confessing to alcohol problems. A knee injury would eventually force his premature retirement having played an important part in helping Swindon out of League Two.

WEDNESDAY 15TH OCTOBER 2003

To the curiosity of geographers, Swindon and Boston United were paired together in the LDV Vans Trophy southern section. The game saw a rare start for the winger Sebastien Ruster, signed cheaply from Cannes, who had gone semi-professional. Cannes later claimed they are entitled to €300,000 in compensation, with Town having to go the Court of Arbitration for Sport to get the sum knocked down to something sensible. Swindon lost 2-1 at York Street, with an injury-time goal from the burly Adebayo Akinfenwa.

WEDNESDAY 16TH OCTOBER 1968

Swindon blew a great chance to knock First Division Coventry City out of the League Cup by surrendering a 2-0 lead at Highfield Road to draw 2-2. Don Rogers put Swindon in front late in the first half by firing in a low shot after being set up by Joe Butler. After Coventry applied more pressure, Swindon reasserted themselves and looked on course to win when Roger Smart drove in Don Heath's knockdown with 20 minutes to go. But Coventry recovered with two goals inside the last four minutes of the tie. Firstly John Tudor scored, then on 88 minutes Tony Hateley's header from a cross meant a fourth-round replay.

THURSDAY 16TH OCTOBER 1986

Lou Macari moved in the transfer market, completing the signing of Oxford United's Mark Jones for £30,000. Jones, a useful midfielder, would only play the one season due to injury. Out of the door went Martin Ling, who had only played four games and not really fitted in with the 'get the ball forward quickly' style that the Town boss preached. He joined Southend, with Town taking a £10,000 loss on the deal having paid £25,000 to bring him in from Exeter City.

WEDNESDAY 16TH OCTOBER 1996

Swindon enjoyed a 6-0 romp over Huddersfield Town in Division One. The six goals arrived in a frenzied 19-minute spell of play, albeit broken up by the half-time whistle. After Mark Walters opened the scoring on 28 minutes Peter Thorne, Wayne Allison (on his birthday) and Kevin Horlock all join in before half-time. Three minutes into the second half, Thorne has scored twice more to make it six, which was when the scoring, slightly prematurely, stopped.

SATURDAY 17TH OCTOBER 1914

Despite Britain being at war, with World War I having started in July, the Southern League season continued as normal. Swindon beat Brighton & Hove Albion 2-1, thanks to two Harold Fleming goals.

SATURDAY 17TH OCTOBER 1981

John Trollope's Swindon side moved to the top of the Division Three table in terrific style by beating Bristol Rovers 4-1 at Eastville. Andy Rowland's double made it 2-0 before the break, with Charlie Henry adding the third and although Archie Stephens pulled one back, Swindon reasserted themselves quickly with a goal through young striker Paul Rideout. Terry Cooper was sacked by Bristol Rovers afterwards, but the encouraging start tailed off alarmingly, with the side not winning again until January.

TUESDAY 17TH OCTOBER 1989

Swindon scored a comprehensive Division Two derby win over Oxford United, with Steve White (2) and Colin Calderwood netting in a 3-0 victory having led 2-0 at half-time. White's first was a lovely placed finish to make the game effectively safe.

SATURDAY 18TH OCTOBER 1980

John Trollope made Football League history as he turned out at left-back in the 1-1 draw with Carlisle United in Division Three. Trollope, aged 37, made his 765th league appearance for Swindon, breaking the record of Portsmouth's Jimmy Dickinson, who offered his congratulations beforehand. Swindon were ten minutes away from keeping a clean sheet before Hugh McAuley equalised for the Cumbrian side.

SATURDAY 19TH OCTOBER 1907

Secretary-manager Sam Allen threw in Harold Fleming for a Southern League debut just a week after he impressed on trial. Fleming responded with a goal in a 4-0 win over Luton Town.

SATURDAY 19TH OCTOBER 1963

Swindon crushed Leyton Orient 5-0 in Division Two, with the goals spread between Ernie Hunt (2), Mike Summerbee, Don Rogers and Keith Morgan. The players had been followed round all week by a BBC regional TV crew, producing a documentary called *Six Days Till Saturday*. They saw Ernie Hunt and Mike Summerbee have a kickaround with children in the street and got under the skin of the club in the build-up to the week's game.

TUESDAY 19TH OCTOBER 1965

Don Rogers scored a hat-trick in just five minutes as Swindon Town inflicted a 6-0 defeat on York City in Division Three. Rogers' goals arrived in the 83rd, 85th and 88th minutes as a tired York defence can't handle his skills. The other goals were from John Trollope, through a penalty, Dennis Brown and Jimmy Lawton.

TUESDAY 19TH OCTOBER 1976

Defender Russell Lewis, now 20, signed his first professional contract, having been spotted playing for the Welsh side based in Bridgend, Everwarm. The centre-back goes on to play more than 200 games for the club, having been involved in just a handful of matches in his first three seasons. Lewis would be a regular in the side that was relegated and played in Division Four, before moving to Northampton Town on a free transfer at the end of the 1982/83 season.

SATURDAY 20TH OCTOBER 1973

Swindon ended a poor run in Division Two by beating Oxford United 1-0 at the County Ground, to give Les Allen's side their first win in nine matches. Striker Richard Legg, signed from Chippenham, got the only goal in what proved to be one of just seven league victories all season. It's also just the third time Town have found the back of the net in that poor run.

TUESDAY 20TH OCTOBER 1981

Three days after beating Bristol Rovers 4-1 to move to the top of Division Three, John Trollope's side showed a complete reversal of form as they lose 5-0 at Walsall, with Saddlers striker Alan Buckley scoring twice. It's not even as if injury or suspension can be blamed, as it was exactly the same starting line-up that took to the field.

MONDAY 21ST OCTOBER 1968

After letting a two-goal lead in the original tie slip, Swindon had no trouble disposing of Division One side Coventry City in their League Cup fourth-round replay. Don Rogers fires in an early goal on ten minutes and six minutes later he set up the second goal, crossing for Roger Smart to double the advantage. It's 3-0 midway through the first half as Willie Penman scored following good work by Peter Noble – and the defence had little trouble seeing off their apparent betters for the rest of the contest, with Peter Downsborough very rarely having to break sweat. The win put Swindon into the last eight of the tournament for the first time.

THURSDAY 21ST OCTOBER 1999

Swindon found a seven-figure offer for striker George Ndah too good to resist, and he completed a £1m move to Wolverhampton Wanderers. Ndah was signed for £500,000 from Crystal Palace and his exceptional pace made him a real threat, especially when he scored 13 goals in the 1998/99 season. Swindon perhaps cashed in at the right time. The unfortunate Ndah broke his leg early into his stint with Wolves and was subsquently plagued with knee problems throughout his career.

TUESDAY 22ND OCTOBER 1985

It was five victories in a row for Lou Macari's Swindon side in Division Four, with Peter Coyne's second-half goal enough to earn a 1-0 win over Stockport County. More than 7,000 fans are inside the County Ground for the match, which doubled the attendance compared to when the run started against Exeter City.

TUESDAY 22ND OCTOBER 2002

The 1,747 fans in attendance were rewarded for their loyalty as they saw Swindon rattle six past Southend United in a Johnstone's Paint Trophy victory. The match was level at 1-1 midway through the first half when striker Graeme Jones equalised, but a goal from the late Jimmy Davis and one from Matt Heywood made it 3-1 before half-time. Danny Invincibile added the fourth just after the break and when Southend's Steve Clark was sent off, manager Andy King was confident enough to make a triple substitution which included goalkeeper Bart Griemink. There were two goals in the last two minutes, a lovely 25-yard shot by Stefani Miglioranzi and one from Sam Parkin.

WEDNESDAY 23RD OCTOBER 1935

Swindon beat Notts County 4-3 in the Division Three South Cup with outside-right Frank Peters scoring a hat-trick. Just 1,814 fans turn up for the contest, staged in the afternoon before the days of floodlights.

TUESDAY 23RD OCTOBER 1979

It's a typical day for Alan Mayes and Andy Rowland. The prolific strike pairing were both on target inside half an hour as Swindon earned a 2-1 win in Division Three over Plymouth Argyle at the County Ground. It's the second victory in a run of four straight league wins.

SATURDAY 23RD OCTOBER 1993

Swindon fans gave former captain Colin Calderwood a tremendous reception at White Hart Lane, as Town faced Spurs in the Premier League. Spurs, who also included David Kerslake in their side, took the lead through Jazon Dozzell. A Paul Bodin penalty midway through the second half earned Swindon a point in the 1-1 draw.

SATURDAY 24TH OCTOBER 1964

Swindon gave former Scottish international goalkeeper Frank Haffey his debut having paid Celtic £7,650 for the man infamous for conceding nine goals in an international with England. Haffey was unable to prevent a 2-1 defeat at Preston North End in Division Two.

TUESDAY 24TH OCTOBER 2006

Swindon appointed youth-team manager David Tuttle as caretaker boss after the departures of Dennis Wise and Gus Poyet to Leeds United. Tuttle turned the role down within 24 hours, saying it had arrived too quickly, despite having been a manager with Millwall. Wise left the club with a parting shot at unnamed individuals on the board, having been brought in by Bill Power and Mark Devlin. Defender Adrian Williams ended up taking over, and he appointed his former team-mate Barry Hunter as his assistant.

SATURDAY 25TH OCTOBER 1969

Swindon missed the presence of Don Rogers on the wing at Fratton Park. Without him, Fred Ford's team were beaten 3-1 by Portsmouth in their Second Division match, with Roger Smart netting the Swindon goal.

FRIDAY 26TH OCTOBER 1923

Future Swindon defender Gareth 'Garth' Hudson was born on this day. He'd go on to play more than 400 games for the club – mostly in the 1950s. The 6' 3" Hudson earned the nickname Garth after a cartoon strip superhero who featured in the *Daily Mirror*.

WEDNESDAY 26TH OCTOBER 1988

For the second season in a row, Swindon managed to blow a lead at Leicester City. This time they ended up with a point from a 3-3 draw, having raced into a 3-0 lead inside half an hour with goals from Phil King, Steve White and Charlie Henry. Steve Foley grabbed a second yellow card seven minutes into the second half. Then Leicester scored three times in ten minutes, with two from Gary McAllister, including a penalty, and a King own goal sandwiched in between. The left-back was then dismissed, with the score at 3-3. Town had to hang on for the last 11 minutes with just nine men.

WEDNESDAY 27TH OCTOBER 2004

Swindon produced an unlikely comeback to beat Sheffield Wednesday 3-2 in League One. Wednesday were 2-0 up with 12 minutes to go, with striker Rory Fallon thrown on in a double substitution. Brian Howard pulled one back with 12 minutes to go. Sam Parkin then equalised with 86 minutes on the clock after good work from Christian Roberts and Sammy Igoe. The Welshman then set up Fallon's winner. He scuffed a shot from the cross, but it bounced up for him to head past the goalkeeper Ola Tidman and complete the turnaround. A point-blank save from Rhys Evans preserved the win.

MONDAY 28TH OCTOBER 1985

Swindon signed goalkeeper Richard Key ahead of their League Cup third-round tie with Sheffield Wednesday. A keeper was urgently required with Scott Endersby unwilling to play. Accounts differ as to exactly why Endersby was unwilling, but he was clearly unhappy with the decision to bring in and play Kenny Allen in front of him, having been the Player of the Year the season before. Swindon claim Enderbsy had demanded a free transfer, which the club was unwilling to give. With Allen cup-tied and Endersby unwilling, manager Lou Macari even contemplates giving Pat Jennings a call before settling on the Brentford man.

SATURDAY 29TH OCTOBER 1904

Swindon won their FA Cup away tie, at home. The match against Whiteheads was switched to the County Ground and Southern League Swindon cruised to a 7-0 victory, with five different scorers.

SATURDAY 29TH OCTOBER 1966

Striker Dennis Brown scored all four goals as Swindon won 4-1 at Bournemouth & Boscombe. Brown, who cost a then club record £15,000 from Chelsea, completed his hat-trick at the start of the second half and made it 4-0 on 57 minutes.

TUESDAY 29TH OCTOBER 1985

With new boy Richard Key in goal, Swindon knocked Division One Sheffield Wednesday out of the FA Cup. Peter Coyne's tenth-minute header from a corner sent Town into the fourth round.

WEDNESDAY 30TH OCTOBER 1968

Swindon faced Derby County at the Baseball Ground in the League Cup quarter-finals. Derby would be tough opponents – managed by Brian Clough and on their way to the Division Two title, with players including Roy McFarland, Dave Mackay, John O'Hare and Kevin Hector. County dominated the game and created numerous chances but Peter Downsborough and company survived – the match finished 0-0 so it was back to the County Ground for a replay.

TUESDAY 30TH OCTOBER 1979

Chic Bates' late goal against Wimbledon puts Swindon into the quarter-finals of the League Cup. Bates, who came on to replace Ian Miller, netted the winner with five minutes to go at Plough Lane to send Swindon through 2-1 and into a quarter-final meeting with Arsenal.

TUESDAY 30TH OCTOBER 2007

Swindon confirmed they have had a transfer embargo placed on them over failure to pay football debts. It's thought around £50,000 was owed to rival clubs and the league stepped in. The dispute further complicated Andrew Fitton's attempts to take over the club. Manager Paul Sturrock was caught in the middle, refusing to blame the current owners, or demand that the prospective ones pay up.

SATURDAY 31ST OCTOBER 1992

Swindon beat Barnsley 1-0 in Division One with an early Craig Maskell penalty. The star of the show was goalkeeper Nicky Hammond, who earned 10/10 ratings in the national media for an outstanding display to keep Barnsley at bay for the remaining 86 minutes of the match.

FRIDAY 31ST OCTOBER 1997

Swindon moved to the top of Division One with a 1-0 win over Portsmouth at Fratton Park, thanks to a goal from Chris Hay from Mark Walters' cross. Steve Mildenhall provided the heroics on his full league debut, carrying on in goal with stitches around his testicles after a heavy collision with Robbie Pethick when going for a loose ball. Mildenhall was only in the side after an injury to Fraser Digby.

SWINDON TOWN
On This Day

NOVEMBER

WEDNESDAY 1st NOVEMBER 1967

Swindon's rising star Don Rogers was included in the England under-23 side who faced Wales at Swansea's Vetch Field – and he scored in a 2-1 win. Rogers' team-mates on the night included Ray Clemence, Emlyn Hughes, John Hollins, Peter Osgood and Brian Kidd.

MONDAY 1st NOVEMBER 1971

Swindon manager Fred Ford left the club, a move that has seemingly been a long time coming. His departure was officially described as a resignation. Ford's side were four points off the relegation zone when the decision was taken and goals had proved hard to come by, with just two in the previous seven games. Having been brought into the club – seemingly over Ford's head – the previous season, Dave Mackay was immediately given the player-manager's role, just short of his 37th birthday. The Scot, an outstanding player and leader of men in his heyday, finds the process of management, at Swindon at least, more challenging.

WEDNESDAY 1st NOVEMBER 1972

Dave Mackay resigned abruptly as manager after a year in the job for 'personal reasons'. The season was proving a struggle, with Swindon again stuck in the lower half of the Division Two table. Mackay's departure followed the sudden sale of Don Rogers, who departed to Crystal Palace and a reunion with his old manager Bert Head, for £147,000, as the costs of building the new North Stand and falling attendances came together in alarming fashion. Mackay's claims of personal reasons seemed hollow when he was almost immediately unveiled as manager of one of the club's Second Division rivals, Nottingham Forest.

SATURDAY 1st NOVEMBER 2008

Striker Simon Cox scored his second hat-trick of the season, but again it was only good enough to earn another point as Swindon drew 3-3 at Scunthorpe United in League One. Cox's first goal put Town 1-0 up and the second levelled the match at 2-2 with a super run and chip from the edge of the area. His final goal was a well-struck penalty, and the equaliser with ten minutes to go, against a side who would go on to win promotion.

SATURDAY 2ND NOVEMBER 1968

Don Rogers was in irresistible form as Swindon trounced Southport 5-1 in Division Three. Rogers scored four times, completing his hat-trick with a penalty before adding a fourth just a minute from time. John Smith got the other goal against the dispirited Sandgrounders, who were no mugs – securing a top-ten finish by the end of the season.

SATURDAY 2ND NOVEMBER 1996

An injury-hit Swindon side pulled off an excellent 2-0 win over Manchester City in Division One with two Wayne Allison goals. It's the first victory over the men from Maine Road in 31 years since a game where Mike Summerbee scored. This match saw his son Nicky's return to the County Ground.

SATURDAY 3RD NOVEMBER 1973

There's a definite thumbs up for new loan signing Peter Eastoe. The 20-year-old striker, an England youth international, was signed on loan from Wolverhampton Wanderers the day before the game. He marks his debut with two goals in a Division Two match with Carlisle United. United's Frank Clarke also grabbed a brace in the 2-2 draw.

SATURDAY 3RD NOVEMBER 1984

Striker Colin Gordon made a dream debut after signing for Swindon from Southern League side Oldbury United. Gordon was thrown on to replace manager Lou Macari in the first half of the Division Four match with Rochdale, and scored the only goal of the game in the second half at Spotland.

SATURDAY 4TH NOVEMBER 1961

Striker Ralph Hunt made it 15 goals for Swindon in just 22 games when he netted in a 2-2 draw with non-league Kettering Town in the FA Cup. Swindon let their grip on the game go though, blowing a 2-0 lead with half an hour to go. Hunt had only arrived in the summer from Grimsby Town, but manager Bert Head decided the 28-year-old was not for him in the long run. After three more matches Hunt was shipped out in December to Port Vale for £3,500.

TUESDAY 4TH NOVEMBER 1975

Swindon were beaten 2-1 by Crystal Palace in a feisty Division Three game at the County Ground. Both sides finished the game with ten men as Swindon goalscorer Dave Moss and Palace winger Peter Taylor were sent off. It made for a challenging evening for referee Jack Taylor, who little more than a year before was in charge of the 1974 World Cup Final.

SATURDAY 4TH NOVEMBER 1978

Swindon beat Southend United 1-0 in Division Three, with striker Paul Gilchrist getting the only goal, his third in just eight games. Gilchrist's finest hour was winning the FA Cup with Southampton but he was unable to hold down a starting place in the side.

TUESDAY 5TH NOVEMBER 1968

The County Ground was a sell out for Swindon's League Cup quarter-final replay with Derby County following the 0-0 draw at the Baseball Ground. The only goal arrived with a slice of luck. Keeper Les Green punched away Owen Dawson's cross, as far as Don Rogers. His shot took a big deflection off Roy McFarland to put Swindon 1-0 in front. Derby had plenty of pressure after the break with Dawson involved again to clear Kevin Hector's goal-bound effort off the line, while Peter Downsborough also produced a vital save with a quarter of an hour of the game left.

MONDAY 5TH NOVEMBER 1990

Swindon signed a World Cup finalist! Argentina defender Nestor Lorenzo, who played in the defeat by Germany in Italia 90, joined the club on an initial loan deal from Bari – teaming up with Ossie Ardiles. With Lorenzo no has-been at the age of 24, the move was regarded as something of a coup for a Second Division side.

THURSDAY 6TH NOVEMBER 1952

Swindon received a handsome £9,000 from First Division Portsmouth for goalkeeper Norman Uprichard. It represented a tidy profit on a player signed for nothing following his release from Arsenal. Uprichard had established himself as Northern Ireland's international keeper at the time, playing in matches with England, Scotland and Wales despite Swindon's place in Division Three (South). He went on to play in the 1958 World Cup.

MONDAY 6TH NOVEMBER 2000

Swindon dispensed with the services of Finnish international centre-back Marko Tuomela, whose loan from Norwegian football ended on this day after playing just four matches. The end for Tuomela came as he was substituted at half-time in a Carling Cup defeat by Tranmere Rovers, with manager Colin Todd singling out the defender for blame for one of the goals and saying he was taken off for "not winning headers".

SATURDAY 7TH NOVEMBER 1987

Swindon let a 2-0 lead slip through their fingers to lose 3-2 to Leicester City, with the Foxes' three goals all coming in the last eight minutes of the match. After Bobby Barnes' early goal, Jimmy Quinn made it 2-0 with three-quarters of the game gone – as he followed up his penalty that was saved by Paul Cooper. Steve Walsh scored the equaliser with a minute to go before defender Mark Venus netted the injury-time winner and the post-match inquest began.

TUESDAY 7TH NOVEMBER 2006

Swindon appointed Scotsman Paul Sturrock as manager to succeed Dennis Wise and Gus Poyet after Adrian Williams' caretaker spell proves not to be a success. Sturrock had only just been dismissed by Sheffield Wednesday. The former Dundee United man had enjoyed success with Plymouth Argyle and Wednesday and his appointment was seen as a wise one. Sturrock brought his usual assistants, Kevin Summerfield and defensive coach John Blackley with him, saying: "Myself and my coaching staff know what it takes to get out of the division. You can't get success overnight but Swindon was a big club and we would like to think that we can start climbing the leagues straight away." His brief was to win immediate promotion.

WEDNESDAY 8TH NOVEMBER 1961

Swindon suffered embarrassment as they were knocked out of the FA Cup by non-league Kettering Town. Town lost 3-0 in what was long-serving keeper Sam Burton's last match for the first team. Bert Head dropped the veteran and replaced him with teenager Mike O'Hara, signed the previous week from Luton Town, with four different keepers eventually used in the league campaign.

SATURDAY 8TH NOVEMBER 1980

An otherwise unmemorable 1-0 defeat at Colchester United in Division Three proved to be of note as it was John Trollope's final appearance for Swindon, leaving his total standing at 770 league games and 889 total appearances for his one professional club. Trollope didn't stop playing due to age, lack of form or fitness, but because he was asked to take over as manager. Without that, Trollope believed he could have played on to the age of 40.

SATURDAY 8TH NOVEMBER 2008

Swindon manager Maurice Malpas came under increasing pressure after an FA Cup exit to non-league Histon. Swindon were beaten 1-0 by the Cambridgeshire side at the tiny Glassworld Stadium, as they couldn't handle the home side's direct style under Steve Fallon and former Cambridge United manager John Beck.

WEDNESDAY 9TH NOVEMBER 1988

Swindon went out of the Simod Cup 2-1 at First Division Norwich City. Swindon trailed 2-0 in the second half thanks to that rarest of things, a goal from future Swindon player Ian Culverhouse. He only scored twice in a career lasting more than 400 matches. A more prolific scorer, Steve White, got a goal back but Swindon went out.

THURSDAY 10TH NOVEMBER 1960

Swindon won a free-scoring FA Cup first-round replay against non-league Bath City at Twerton Park, coming through 6-4 after leading 4-1 at one stage. Bronco Layne scored four times, with the other two goals coming from Ernie Hunt.

SATURDAY 10TH NOVEMBER 1984

Manager Lou Macari had an indication of the task ahead as he plays in a 4-0 defeat at Northampton Town in Division Four. By the end of next season, only two of the starting line-up will still be players at the club.

SATURDAY 10TH NOVEMBER 1990

Nestor Lorenzo's debut attracted a crowd of 8,621 to the County Ground and the Argentinean scored after 29 minutes to start things off in a 3-0 win over Portsmouth. Steve Foley and Duncan Shearer got the other goals.

SATURDAY 11TH NOVEMBER 1939

Although war has been declared, football continued in the wartime league. Swindon drew 2-2 at home with Cardiff City, with Alan Fowler among the goals.

TUESDAY 11TH NOVEMBER 1997

Despite leading Division One and being in contention for promotion to the Premier League, Swindon found an £800,000 offer for striker Wayne Allison too good to resist and he was sold to a Huddersfield side struggling at the foot of the table. The Chief's contract was up at the end of the season and Town were unwilling to risk him leaving on a Bosman free transfer. He would finish up with a highly respectable 36 goals in 120 games and a Division Two championship medal during his time in Wiltshire.

SATURDAY 12TH NOVEMBER 1881

The Spartans and the fascinatingly named St. Mark's Young Men's Friendly Society drew 2-2 and the teams were sufficiently impressed with each other to merge afterwards in what was regarded as the formation of the club, though the name doesn't become Swindon Town for another two years. There are arguments though, that the club began in 1879, according to historian Paul Plowman.

SATURDAY 12TH NOVEMBER 1949

Swindon succumbed to a 3-0 defeat at Notts County in Division Three (South), but there was every excuse as goalkeeper Frank Boulton suffered a broken leg in the days before substitutes were available. The defence also had to deal with the great Tommy Lawton – the England international scored a hat-trick.

WEDNESDAY 12TH NOVEMBER 1980

John Trollope was given the chance to manage the club after the departure of Bobby Smith and a Danny Williams caretaker spell. After much thought he accepted the challenge, albeit after being given assurances that he could return to his position as youth-team coach if things went wrong. Trollope was definitely ambivalent about whether or not to accept, preferring his work developing players, but eventually he did accept. On reflection, he has described taking the post as his "worst decision in football".

TUESDAY 12TH NOVEMBER 2002

Kidderminster and Swindon Town played their LDV Vans Southern Area match at Aggborough – eventually. A power cut meant the match eventually started at around 9pm, before inevitably making its way into extra time with the score 2-2. The game ended on 105 minutes thanks to a golden goal from the Harriers defender Abdou Sall, which came just after 11pm.

SATURDAY 13TH NOVEMBER 1965

Swindon had little trouble disposing of non-league opposition in the first round of the FA Cup, beating Merthyr Tydfil 5-1 at the County Ground. Striker Keith East, signed from Portsmouth, hit four of the five goals against the Welsh side, with the other coming from Roger Smart.

FRIDAY 13TH NOVEMBER 1987

Swindon signed goalkeeper Tim Flowers on loan from Southampton for the second time as cover for Fraser Digby. The future England international had already played twice for Lou Macari in the previous season, but the 20-year-old can't keep a clean sheet in five games.

SATURDAY 14TH NOVEMBER 1964

Swindon were beaten by a Francis Lee-inspired Bolton Wanderers in Division Two, going down to a 3-1 defeat at the County Ground. Lee scored twice, as did Wyn Davies. Swindon's goalscorer was John Trollope, who was on penalty-taking duty.

FRIDAY 14TH NOVEMBER 2008

Manager Maurice Malpas left Swindon, with the departure officially described as by "mutual consent". It followed exits from the FA Cup at Histon and the Johnstone's Paint Trophy at Brighton & Hove Albion, with the board having placed particular emphasis on doing well in cup competitions. Chairman Andrew Fitton described it as; "One of the most difficult decisions I have had to make." Fitton faced some criticism having made the slightly leftfield choice as his first managerial appointment since taking over. The Scot never seemed particularly happy with the media aspect of his role. His tenure lasted just 42 games, resulting in 13 wins, 11 draws and 18 defeats.

SATURDAY 15TH NOVEMBER 1958

Swindon scored one of a number of big wins over Aldershot. This time it was a 5-0 victory in the first round of the FA Cup, with long-serving outside-left Arnold Darcy scoring three times.

WEDNESDAY 15TH NOVEMBER 1972

Swindon striker Ray Treacy was among the most popular men in Ireland. Treacy fired in the winner for the Republic of Ireland against France in a World Cup qualifier in Dublin to give the Irish some hope of making the finals for the first time. The Irish won 2-1, but ended up finishing second in their group behind the Soviet Union and missed out on a trip to Germany.

TUESDAY 15TH NOVEMBER 1994

Swindon played what proved to be their final game in the competition they were responsible for creating, the Anglo-Italian Cup. John Gorman's side visited Serie B side Ascoli and lost 3-1, finding a gangly German striker particularly difficult to handle. Oliver Bierhoff ended up getting a hat-trick. Swindon's goal came via a Chris Hamon penalty.

SATURDAY 16TH NOVEMBER 1957

More than 21,000 crammed into Elm Park for an FA Cup first-round match between Swindon and Reading. The Royals edged through to the second round with a 1-0 win.

SATURDAY 16TH NOVEMBER 1968

While Swindon have been beating the big names in their run in the League Cup, they very nearly got a taste of giant-killing in the first round of the FA Cup, with a crowd of more than 14,000 crammed in to watch Town take on Canterbury City in Kent. A replay looked likely until Don Rogers converted an 89th-minute penalty to send Swindon through to round two.

THURSDAY 16TH NOVEMBER 1995

Steve McMahon signed a player in his own image when he brought in feisty, tough-tackling Scottish midfielder Lee Collins. He cost £15,000 from Albion Rovers.

SATURDAY 17TH NOVEMBER 1945

Swindon played in a two-legged FA Cup tie for the first and only time in the competition's history. Welshman Don Emery, a defender pushed up front, scored the only goal at the County Ground against Bristol Rovers to give Swindon a 1-0 lead to take back to Eastville for the second leg. It proved not to be enough, with Swindon beaten 4-1 in the return game.

SATURDAY 17TH NOVEMBER 1962

Swindon manager Bert Head continued his policy of playing youngsters as he threw in 17-year-old Don Rogers for his debut in a Division Three game with Southend United. The winger didn't score, but he clearly did something right as Town scored a comfortable 4-1 win, with Jack Smith scoring twice inside ten minutes, assisted by goals from Mike Summerbee and Cliff Jackson.

SATURDAY 17TH NOVEMBER 1990

Ossie Ardiles' side lost 2-1 at Sheffield Wednesday – the side who Swindon would have replaced in Division One if they had not been denied promotion. Swindon's goal was an Alan McLoughlin consolation in injury time, while future management duo Danny Wilson and Peter Shirtliff both play for the Owls.

THURSDAY 18TH NOVEMBER 1993

John Gorman signed a new striker with Swindon still looking for a first win in the Premier League since promotion. He paid Wycombe Wanderers £300,000 for 26-year-old forward Keith Scott. Scott had established a good reputation in helping the Buckinghamshire side into the league, but the move represented a big test of his abilities.

SATURDAY 19TH NOVEMBER 1983

Swindon gained handsome revenge against Kettering in the FA Cup, 22 years after they were knocked out of the competition at Rockingham Road. This time they won 7-0 against the non-leaguers. Defender Simon Gibson, signed from Chelsea, scored early from a corner. Jimmy Quinn made it two before the break as Kettering couldn't clear another set-piece. Quinn bagged a second, while Andy Rowland, Charlie Henry, Paul Batty and Leigh Barnard also scored to provide one of the highlights of Ken Beamish's season in charge.

THURSDAY 20TH NOVEMBER 1924

League Cup-winning manager Danny Williams was born on this day in Thrybergh in South Yorkshire. Williams would have three spells in the manager's seat, one as caretaker, while also acting as general manager until 1985, meaning his time at the club would span over three different decades, with a non-stop spell from 1974 to 1985. He would take charge of more than 450 games including his caretaker stint in 1980. At the time of writing he had retired and was living contentedly in Bournemouth.

FRIDAY 20TH NOVEMBER 1964

With Swindon continuing to struggle in Division Two, manager Bert Head broke the club's record transfer fee by paying Chelsea £15,000 for Dennis Brown, who could play at inside-right or left. Brown can't save Swindon from the drop, but he does score 44 goals in 106 games before leaving in 1967 for Northampton Town in a swap deal with Bobby Jones.

SATURDAY 20TH NOVEMBER 1965

Just a week after hitting four goals in the FA Cup win over Merthyr Tydfil, Keith East went one better. East bags five in a 6-2 Division Three win against Mansfield Town. East scored twice before half-time, with his last three goals coming in a 16-minute purple patch in the second half. East was the only player to achieve the feat for Swindon since World War II.

WEDNESDAY 20TH NOVEMBER 1968

Swindon gave themselves a real chance of a first visit to Wembley by beating Division One side Burnley 2-1 at Turf Moor in the first leg of their League Cup semi-final. Swindon started brightly and had a goal disallowed, before Burnley lost their centre-back Colin Waldron with a broken jaw. Town opened the scoring with a well-worked free kick, with John Smith's ball knocked down by Peter Noble for Stan Harland to fire in. Midway through the second half, the Clarets equalised through Ralph Coates, but Swindon reclaimed the lead immediately when Don Rogers' through-ball was met by Peter Noble before keeper Harry Thomson could get there. It's a superb result against a side on a fine run of form in the First Division.

TUESDAY 21st NOVEMBER 1973

With the team struggling and finances poor, another of the 1969 League Cup heroes was sold, with Welsh international Rod Thomas off to Derby County for £100,000. The move saw Thomas link up with his old boss Dave Mackay. Bert Head had paid just £500 for him from Gloucester City. Thomas would go on to win Division One with Derby County but would still describe the League Cup win at Wembley as his happiest moment in football.

TUESDAY 21st NOVEMBER 1989

Swindon beat Bolton Wanderers 2-1 after extra time to finally end a marathon League Cup tie which has gone to a third replay and taken almost a month to complete, with the initial match on October 24th. The original tie had finished 3-3, then there were two 1-1 draws at Burnden Park, both after extra time. The teams were just three minutes away from a fourth replay before Ross MacLaren's deflected long-range shot finally settled matters after around seven-and-a-half hours of football.

MONDAY 21st NOVEMBER 1994

The board took the decision to sack manager John Gorman, with some fans calling for his head during the local-derby defeat at Bristol City. It's a fourth straight defeat which has seen Town, who had been in the top six in the early weeks of the season, drop into a disconcerting 16th place in the Division One table.

SATURDAY 22nd NOVEMBER 1980

Swindon were pushed hard by non-league Weymouth in the first round of the FA Cup before coming through 3-2 at the County Ground. Swindon were 2-1 down midway through the second half, before a goal from Russell Lewis and a late winner from Chris Kamara restored the natural order.

SATURDAY 22nd NOVEMBER 2003

Striker Sam Parkin got a goal against the club he supported as a boy when Swindon drew 1-1 with QPR at the County Ground, with both sides looking for promotion out of Division Two.

SATURDAY 23RD NOVEMBER 1974

The FA Cup gives Reading, in Division Four, a chance to meet their Division Three neighbours Swindon at the County Ground, the first time the teams had met in six years. A crowd of 13, 365 saw the higher division side score a comprehensive 4-0 win, through Trevor Anderson, Peter Eastoe, a Dave Moss penalty and an own goal.

TUESDAY 23RD NOVEMBER 1999

Promising youngster Michael Carrick, 18, gets his first goal in professional football. The midfielder, on loan from West Ham United, scored in Swindon's 2-1 home defeat by Charlton Athletic in Division One. Carrick has since gone on to join Manchester United for more than £18m and won more than 20 England caps.

WEDNESDAY 24TH NOVEMBER 1965

Don Rogers' talents were recognised at England under-23 level for the first time. Rogers played for England in a 2-1 win over Yugoslavia at The Dell. Alongside him was a familiar face, Ernie Hunt – his former Swindon colleague was now a Wolves player.

SATURDAY 24TH NOVEMBER 1973

Swindon got their only home win over Aston Villa, to date, when Dave Moss scored in a 1-0 victory in Division Two.

WEDNESDAY 24TH NOVEMBER 1993

Finally, Swindon got their first top-flight win – and they did it with ten men after Luc Nijholt was sent off inside the first 20 minutes. Keith Scott got the only goal with a first-half header as Swindon beat QPR 1-0 at the County Ground but manage to hang on for the remainder of the game. It came at the 16th time of asking.

MONDAY 25TH NOVEMBER 1963

Swindon found Division One West Ham United too strong for them in a League Cup fourth-round replay at Upton Park. Having held them at the County Ground, Town go out, losing 4-1 with Geoff Hurst and John Byrne among the scorers. Don Rogers got the Swindon goal.

SATURDAY 26TH NOVEMBER 1966

Swindon played Horsham at Queen's Street in the Sussex side's first-ever appearance in the first-round proper of the FA Cup. Town made sure there was no joy for the locals with Don Rogers, Mel Nurse and Dennis Brown scoring in a 3-0 win.

MONDAY 26TH NOVEMBER 1984

Lou Macari suffered embarrassment early into his managerial career when Swindon were beaten 2-1 at home by Dagenham in an FA Cup first-round replay. Alan Mayes put Swindon ahead, but with a second replay looming deep in extra time, Les Whitton's goal was enough to cause a shock and make Macari consider the futures of several of the squad very carefully.

SATURDAY 27TH NOVEMBER 1954

Swindon and Southampton drew 1-1 at The Dell in Division Three (South), with midfielder Jim Cross getting his first goal of the season. It was still just one win away from home for Maurice Lindley's side since the start of the season.

SATURDAY 28TH NOVEMBER 1925

Swindon record their biggest-ever FA Cup win, with a 10-1 slaughter of Farnham United Breweries. It was 7-0 at half-time. Frank 'Swerver' Richardson scored four times, Jack Johnson helped himself to a hat-trick, with Bertie Denyer getting two and Alec Wall one.

MONDAY 28TH NOVEMBER 1994

After the departure of John Gorman, Swindon decided to go down the player-manager route – which had worked so effectively with Lou Macari, Ossie Ardiles and Glenn Hoddle – by choosing Steve McMahon as his successor. McMahon came with an impressive CV littered with honours at Liverpool, and England international caps. He also represented a different type of character than John Gorman, as he was known as a pretty uncompromising, hard-tackling, defensive midfielder. McMahon quickly says he intends to carry on playing as he's still just 33 when appointed. The Scouser would fail to really win a place in the hearts of Swindon fans, despite leading the side to the Division Two title in some style following relegation the previous season.

SATURDAY 29TH NOVEMBER 1980

Striker Paul Rideout became the youngest player in Swindon history when he made his debut against Hull City at the age of 16 years, 107 days. He beat Ernie Hunt's record by 75 days in the process. Rideout, who had looked outstanding in England schoolboy internationals, played for the full 90 minutes. He then scored right at the end of a 3-1 win to vindicate manager John Trollope's faith in him.

SUNDAY 29TH NOVEMBER 1992

Swindon drew 3-3 in a dramatic televised game with Peterborough United in Division One. Shaun Taylor scored at both ends, while Swindon looked on course for a win until Nicky Hammond's terrible clearance presented Tony Adcock with the chance to equalise for the Posh six minutes from time.

SATURDAY 30TH NOVEMBER 1974

Dave Moss hit a hat-trick, including two penalties, while Peter Eastoe also netted as Swindon saw off Colchester United 4-1 in Division Three. It was an unhappy return for United defender Ray Bunkell, who Swindon manager Les Allen had let leave the County Ground the previous season.

THURSDAY 30TH NOVEMBER 1989

Full-back Phil King was sold to First Division side Sheffield Wednesday with Swindon collecting a then club record £400,000 for the transfer. Town also netted an extra £50,000 in appearance clauses. King had completed a successful month's loan with the Owls before making the move permanent with Paul Bodin slotting into his place. More than seven years later, King would return, signed by Steve McMahon on a free transfer.

WEDNESDAY 30TH NOVEMBER 1994

Although Steve McMahon had been appointed, Andy Rowland picked the team for Swindon's League Cup fourth-round tie with Derby County. With Swindon at home, he took a positive approach, playing three strikers in Jan Age Fjortoft, Keith Scott and Andy Mutch. Rowland's team were able to pull off a 2-1 win to move into the quarter-finals. Fjortoft scored early and late, getting the winner with six minutes to go in between a strike by Mark Stallard.

SWINDON TOWN
On This Day

DECEMBER

SATURDAY 1st DECEMBER 1973

Swindon came up against Don Rogers for the first time since his controversial sale to Crystal Palace. Rogers, wearing the number 11 shirt, was predictably on target at Selhurst Park as Swindon were beaten 4-2, with Peter Taylor among the other scorers for Palace. Strikers Peter Eastoe and Dave Syrett got the Swindon goals.

SATURDAY 1st DECEMBER 1987

Winger Bobby Barnes scored for the sixth league game in a row, as Swindon beat a struggling Huddersfield Town side 4-1 in Division Two. Barnes was signed for £50,000 from Aldershot Town, with Steve Berry going the other way. The midfielder would fail to hold down a consistent place in the team in the latter half of the season though, eventually being sold on to Bournemouth.

SATURDAY 2nd DECEMBER 1950

Swindon got the better of Bristol City in a Division Three (South) derby at the County Ground. Inside-left Joe Simner scored the goal, the last of his 13 in two seasons at the club before being released and joining non-league Bedford.

SUNDAY 2nd DECEMBER 1984

Swindon lost 1-0 at promotion-chasing Darlington in Division Four. The idea of Sunday football was clearly popular, with a crowd of more than 6,000 at Feethams.

SATURDAY 3rd DECEMBER 1949

Swindon had a free-scoring day against Exeter City, recording a 7-1 win over the Grecians in Division Three (South). There are braces for Harry Lunn, Maurice Owen and Jimmy Bain. Outside-left Bain would be a regular for six seasons, notching up 43 goals in 255 appearances.

SATURDAY 3rd DECEMBER 1966

Swindon and Oldham Athletic serve up nine goals for a 10,000-plus crowd at the County Ground for their Division Three match. Don Rogers was naturally at the centre of things with a hat-trick completed in the 87th minute. Dennis Brown and Bruce Walker also score. That all came after ex-Swindon forward Frank Large gave Oldham the lead.

SATURDAY 3RD DECEMBER 1994

Steve McMahon's first match in charge of Swindon perhaps proved an indication of things to come. McMahon picked himself in midfield for the trip to Southend United and saw his side go 1-0 down inside the opening five minutes. Defender Andy Edwards then scored the second for the Essex side, before a McMahon tackle earned him a second yellow card after an early booking.

SATURDAY 4TH DECEMBER 1965

Swindon won 6-1 at Grantham Town in the FA Cup second round, after the game was goalless at half-time. Five different scorers chipped in – Roger Smart with two, plus Ernie Weaver, Mel Nurse, Dennis Brown and Keith East.

WEDNESDAY 4TH DECEMBER 1968

It's a sell-out as Burnley visit the County Ground, with Swindon looking to hold on to their 2-1 first-leg lead in the semi-finals of the League Cup, with Wembley tantalisingly close. Despite being the away side, the First Division team dominated the first half and they level the tie on aggregate on 50 minutes through Frank Casper. Shortly afterwards, the Clarets seize the lead when Peter Downsborough can only palm a cross straight to Steve Kindon. It meant Burnley led 3-2 on aggregate. Their advantage only lasted six minutes though, as Don Rogers' corner was headed in by John Smith. Swindon then got close to closing the contest out when Roger Smart had a shot cleared off the line. With the aggregate score tied at 3-3, the game went into extra time. Although Swindon had the edge, neither side could score. With the penalty shoot-out yet to be invented, it's decided the two sides must meet in a third match at a neutral venue.

TUESDAY 4TH DECEMBER 1979

Another big night was in store for Swindon in the League Cup as Bobby Smith's Third Division side travelled to Arsenal in the quarter finals. Swindon fell behind early, to an Alan Sunderland penalty, and time was running out when Bobby Smith made a change, taking off Brian Williams and bringing on centre-back Billy Tucker. The sub popped up to head in a corner with eight minutes left, and Swindon earned a replay.

TUESDAY 5TH DECEMBER 2006

Paul Sturrock saw his Swindon side lose for the first time since taking charge, as they are beaten 2-0 at Mansfield Town in League Two. Sturrock criticised the performance of his forwards, bar youngster Lukas Jutkiewicz, despite the fact that defensive mistakes led to both goals.

SATURDAY 6TH DECEMBER 1930

Striker Harry Morris was in his customary poaching form, with the club's all-time record scorer netting twice in a 4-0 Division Three (South) win over Torquay United. It meant Morris hit double figures, with the first goal his tenth of the season – sluggish by his own standards. He even had a five-game run without a goal. Morris doubters, though, are proved wrong – he finished with 35 goals in 40 league matches.

TUESDAY 6TH DECEMBER 1977

Attacking midfielder Roy Carter joined Swindon, costing £22,000 from Hereford United. He would go on to become club captain, making more than 200 appearances and scoring 39 goals. He would, however, be part of the squad relegated to Division Four for the first time in club history, where his penalty taking would let him down in a key game with Newport County.

THURSDAY 6TH DECEMBER 1979

Manager Bobby Smith was given some of the proceeds of the run to the League Cup quarter-finals to spend, and he splashed out £110,000 on midfielder Glenn Cockerill from Lincoln City. He would struggle at the County Ground, though, and not see eye-to-eye with John Trollope when he took over. Cockerill would half prove Bobby Smith right later in his career, becoming a big success in the top division with Southampton.

SATURDAY 7TH DECEMBER 1957

Striker Bill Roost grabbed a hat-trick in a 3-1 Division Three (South) game at Shrewsbury Town. They were his first goals since being signed from Bristol Rovers for £2,000 in the close season. They were also his last, as Roost failed to score again in 14 more games before being let go at the end of the 1958/59 season.

SATURDAY 7TH DECEMBER 1968

Three year after their 6-1 romp at Grantham Town in the FA Cup, Swindon were drawn away to the Lincolnshire side again. This time the game at London Road was much closer. Swindon snatched a win with goals in the last ten minutes from Chris Jones and John Smith, who net within a minute.

WEDNESDAY 8TH DECEMBER 1897

Striker Cecil Blakemore was born. Blakemore spent just one season at Swindon, when he was signed in July 1933. At 35, he was given the task of replacing the prolific Harry Morris. Blakemore scored just eight times and was released at the end of the campaign.

SATURDAY 8TH DECEMBER 1979

Swindon recorded their biggest post-war win, as Bobby Smith, Brian Williams and Andy Rowland go to town, coming up with an 8-0 victory against their former club Bury. Rowland scored twice, as did Ray McHale and Rowland's strike partner Alan Mayes. Chris Kamara and Billy Tucker were the others to net, with the four goals split evenly between the first half and the second. Among the shell-shocked Bury midfield contingent was a 19-year-old Danny Wilson. The victory lifted Swindon into the top three in the Third Division.

SATURDAY 9TH DECEMBER 1961

Bert Head's youth policy could clearly be seen in the side that took to the field in a Division Three match with Southend United. The side included five teenagers; the goalkeeper Mike O'Hara, both full-backs Terry Wollen and John Trollope, plus Mike Summerbee and Ernie Hunt. Another defender, Keith Morgan, was just 21. The game finished 0-0.

SATURDAY 9TH DECEMBER 2006

Swindon travelled to the League Two leaders Walsall, who had dropped just two points at the Bescot Stadium all season. That changed after Swindon produced an excellent performance to win 2-0. Young striker Lukas Jutkiewicz got his first goal in a Town shirt when he finished off a through-ball from Michael Timlin. Jutkiewicz also won a second-half penalty that Christian Roberts converted to round things off.

THURSDAY 10TH DECEMBER 1959

Inside-left Bob Edwards and inside-right John Richards left Swindon for a combined fee of £6,000, joining Third Division rivals Norwich City. The pair went on to clinch promotion as the Canaries finished second. Edwards left after having a very respectable scoring record in a side that had generally struggled in Division Three (South), scoring 69 times in 185 matches in some of the bleakest seasons in the Football League.

SATURDAY 10TH DECEMBER 1983

Swindon pulled off a minor cup shock, when they travelled as a Fourth Division side to Millwall, who were mid-table in Division Three. Swindon recovered from being 2-1 down to lead 3-2 as Jimmy Quinn and Paul Batty scored, and they moved into round three despite playing the last 11 minutes with ten men after defender Simon Gibson's sending off.

TUESDAY 11TH DECEMBER 1979

Swindon beat Arsenal 4-3 in the League Cup quarter-finals in one of the greatest and most incident-filled matches seen at the County Ground. Swindon took hold of the game quickly, grabbing two-goal lead inside the first 20 minutes. They were given plenty of help with the first goal, when Brian Williams' deep left-wing cross was headed into his own net by Arsenal defender Steve Walford, with no Swindon player in sight. Next, Alan Mayes shot from the edge of the area and managed to beat Pat Jennings with a looping effort. It stayed that way until the hour mark, when Liam Brady scored. Four minutes later, Arsenal help out again. Chris Kamara's shot from a corner was blocked, and he headed the rebound back towards goal. Defender John Hollins managed not only to block Pat Jennings route to the ball, but flick it past his keeper for a second own goal. Arsenal showed their quality with a second Liam Brady goal and with just six minutes left, Brian Talbot equalised to send the match into extra time. There were minutes left when Swindon won a free kick and pumped it into the box. Graham Rix's clearing header was not the strongest, and Chris Kamara had another shot, which was half-cleared into the path of Andy Rowland. He drilled the ball home and put Swindon into the last four, ten years after their run to the final. First Division Wolves awaited.

SATURDAY 11TH DECEMBER 1993

Swindon came desperately close to getting their first away win in the Premier League – at Anfield. Swindon were twice ahead, firstly when John Moncur slid in to finish off a great team passing move, and again when Keith Scott eventually fired home after a melee inside the box. With just six minutes to go, Liverpool swung over a corner and Mark Wright won the header. Fraser Digby looked to have it covered, but it slipped through his fingers and Swindon hade to settle for a pleasing, yet frustrating, 2-2 draw.

SATURDAY 12TH DECEMBER 1925

Frank Richardson, who has the wonderful nickname of 'Swerver', scored four times as Swindon go through to the third round of the FA Cup with a 7-0 won over Sittingbourne at the County Ground. The other goals came from Bertie Davies (2) and Bertie Denyer.

TUESDAY 12TH DECEMBER 1967

There's an all-Wiltshire affair in the FA Cup, as Swindon met Salisbury City at the County Ground in the first round. Swindon scored a comfortable 4-0 win, with free-scoring striker Pat Terry getting a hat-trick. The other goal came from Willie Penman.

SATURDAY 12TH DECEMBER 1970

Swindon drew 1-1 with Leyton Orient in a home game in Division Two. The O's defender Terry Mancini looked like a precursor to Shaun Taylor, as he played the entire game – and scored – while wearing a gumshield to protect his broken teeth. The Swindon goal came from Chris Porter, signed from Bridgwater Town.

THURSDAY 13TH DECEMBER 1990

Midfielder Alan McLoughlin became the first £1m player in Swindon history when he was sold to Division One Southampton. The club said they had little option, with manager Ossie Ardiles telling HTV; "We are selling because, at the moment, we owe a lot of money. I didn't want to sell him and am disappointed." Ardiles doesn't know if he will see any of the money reinvested into the squad.

SATURDAY 13TH DECEMBER 2003

Swindon lost a dramatic match against promotion rivals Plymouth Argyle in Division Two. Trailing 2-0 with ten minutes to go, Swindon pulled a goal back when Rory Fallon managed to knee home a corner. In the last minute, it looked as if they'd rallied for a point, when Andy Gurney's free kick broke to Sam Parkin, who finished from close range. But Steve Robinson was sent off for picking up a second booking, and Plymouth exploited the ten men and some uncertain defending with Marino Keith scoring an injury-time winner.

FRIDAY 14TH DECEMBER 1934

Swindon were beaten 7-4 by Watford at Vicarage Road in Division Three (South). Alan Fowler notched a hat-trick in a losing cause, with Harry Bowl scoring Swindon's other goal. Watford's Billy Lane was happier with his three goals.

TUESDAY 14TH DECEMBER 1982

Division Four Swindon beat Brentford, who were in Division Three, in a lively FA Cup second-round replay at Griffin Park. Both sides played the majority of the game with ten men after Kevin Baddeley and Terry Hurlock were sent off when they clashed. Andy Rowland levels the tie midway through the second half and Swindon proved the stronger side, with a goal from Howard Pritchard in extra time, before Paul Batty rounded things off right at the end of the match to put Swindon into the third-round draw.

TUESDAY 15TH DECEMBER 1942

Arguably the most successful of 'Bert's Babes' was born on this day, when Mike Summerbee was brought into the world in Preston. He was spotted playing for Cheltenham Town as a teenager, before making his debut at the age of 17. Summerbee would continue to grow and grow, becoming a first-team regular, helping Swindon into the Second Division and winning England under-23 caps, playing as a traditional out-and-out winger who would supply a stream of quality crosses. When he was sold on to Manchester City, he would be the first and only one of Bert Head's prodigies to win full England honours, as well as winning the First Division with Manchester City.

TUESDAY 15TH DECEMBER 1981

Swindon just edged past non-league Sutton United at the County Ground to make the third round of the FA Cup. Striker Micky Joyce put Sutton in front, with Roy Carter equalising just before half-time. Everything looked set for a replay before Howard Pritchard scored a winner in injury time.

SATURDAY 15TH DECEMBER 2007

Things felt bleak on and off the pitch as Swindon were beaten 3-0 by Brighton & Hove Albion at the County Ground in League One. There was no permanent manager with Dave Byrne continuing in caretaker charge. Striker Kaid Mohamed – played out wide – was so poor he was substituted before half-time, while the club threatened to fall into a black hole as Andrew Fitton's consortium negotiated desperately to complete their takeover against a board who were not showing a huge willingness to sell. Fans made their feelings clear by chanting "There's only one Andrew Fitton" before kick-off.

SATURDAY 16TH DECEMBER 1961

Swindon came back from conceding in the first minute to get a 2-2 draw with Portsmouth in their Division Three game at Fratton Park. Ernie Hunt, with his eighth of the season, and Bill Atkins scored both goals in a five-minute period of the second half.

SATURDAY 16TH DECEMBER 1995

Swindon drew 1-1 at home with Wrexham, their bogey side in Division Two that season. The game exhibited the pattern of many that season, with the visiting side coming to defend. Wayne O'Sullivan broke through with 14 minutes to go, but close to injury time Wrexham got a penalty, which was converted by Karl Connolly.

SATURDAY 17TH DECEMBER 1938

Goals from Ben Morton and Arthur Barraclough gave Swindon a 2-1 win in an all West Country affair with Exeter City in Division Three (South). It's Morton's 18th goal of the season, with the striker showing the lethal form that made him the club's first £1,000 signing the season before. World War II robbed him of a chance to really show what he could do.

SUNDAY 17TH DECEMBER 1989

Swindon got an amazing win at West Bromwich Albion in Division Two when the Baggies had collective brain fade from the penalty spot. Swindon scored early, when Duncan Shearer finished after Alan McLoughlin's shot was palmed out to him by the keeper. Steve White's header then made it 2-0 after Shearer had hit the post earlier. West Brom then won a penalty when Colin Calderwood tangled with Chris Whyte, but Fraser Digby comfortably kept out Bernard McNally's effort. Within seconds, there was another spot kick. As Swindon tried to clear the resulting corner, Duncan Shearer was judged to have handled the ball. Graham Harbey had a go this time, and sent the ball high over the bar. West Brom got a third penalty in four minutes following Jon Gittens' challenge. Don Goodman scored but Town held on for a 2-1 victory.

SATURDAY 18TH DECEMBER 1926

Harry Morris was at his goal-poaching best, scoring five times in a 6-2 home win over Queens Park Rangers in Division Three (South).

WEDNESDAY 18TH DECEMBER 1968

Swindon and Burnley replayed their League Cup semi-final with the game staged at the neutral venue of The Hawthorns. Swindon dominated the first half of the contest, and were in front inside the first ten minutes when John Smith scored from the edge of the area. Burnley were by far the stronger side in the second half, with Peter Downsborough being forced into three high quality saves to preserve the Swindon lead. In the last minute their pressure paid as Dave Thomas smacked home a free kick that had fallen to him in the penalty area. Swindon fans feared the worst as the Clarets then scored right at the start of extra time when Frank Casper linked up with Ralph Coates. Despite all this, Danny Williams' side didn't buckle and they got a helping foot from full-back Arthur Bellamy whose sliced clearance became an own goal. Four minutes later came the goal that sent Swindon to Wembley, as Peter Noble, a future Claret, fired in the winner to complete the run to the final which had seen them beat two sides from Division One and two more from Division Two. Arsenal awaited in March's final.

SATURDAY 19TH DECEMBER 1964

Swindon's hopes of escaping relegation from Division Two looked a lot brighter after a 3-0 win at Leyton Orient. It's the second victory in a row and new signing Dennis Brown took centre-stage, with the club-record purchase scoring a 52-minute hat-trick at Brisbane Road.

FRIDAY 19TH DECEMBER 1986

Striker Jimmy Quinn returned to the County Ground for a second spell, with Swindon paying Blackburn Rovers £50,000. He'd been sold to the Lancashire club for £32,500 two-and-a-half years before. The Ulsterman scored 12 goals in the second half of the season to help lift Swindon to back-to-back promotions.

SATURDAY 20TH DECEMBER 1924

Swindon enjoyed one of a number of big wins over Merthyr Town they would have during the Welsh side's stay in the Football League. Swindon won 5-1 in Wales with Frank Richardson (3) and Jack Johnson (2) the scorers.

SUNDAY 20TH DECEMBER 1992

As was traditional, Swindon suffered a defeat and a sending off at Filbert Street. This time it's less of a hard luck story as Leicester raced into a 3-0 lead inside the opening half-hour. Micky Hazard pulled one back early in the second half, before David Lowe made it 4-1. Colin Calderwood was then dismissed for picking up two yellow cards in 12 minutes, before a late own goal from Steve Walsh made the final scoreline 4-2.

THURSDAY 20TH DECEMBER 2001

Swindon director of football Roy Evans decided to leave the club having only been appointed in the summer. It followed months of boardroom infighting as Danny Donegan and his colleagues were ousted by a consortium involving the former champion jockey Willie Carson. Carson and fellow director Bob Holt outlined the finances to Evans, who thought he was no longer in a position to move the club towards the First Division. The future of Neil Ruddock was less clear, with assistant Malcolm Crosby seen as the early favourite to take over the job.

SATURDAY 21st DECEMBER 1889

In a game reflecting a different era, Swindon scored a 4-1 win in a home friendly against the Oxford College Servants.

TUESDAY 21st DECEMBER 1976

Swindon had another narrow escape against non-league opposition in the FA Cup, squeezing past Hitchin Town in a second-round replay at the County Ground. Town need extra time to see off their opponents 3-1 with Dave Moss (2) and Dave Syrett providing relief as much as joy with the goals.

FRIDAY 21st DECEMBER 1990

Manager Ossie Ardiles was allowed to invest some of the money raised by the sale of Alan McLoughlin back into the squad, so he paid Bari a reported £400,000 for Argentinean defender Nestor Lorenzo after his loan spell proved to be a success. The fee was a club record.

FRIDAY 21st DECEMBER 2001

The man dismissed to make way for Roy Evans made a dramatic return as manager, with Andy King returning for a second spell in charge. Although the formalities were not complete, King watched Swindon lose 3-1 in a poor performance at Notts County, where Neil Ruddock was sent off. The board said they felt King could work within the budget, or lack of it – in contrast to Evans. King's return was not welcomed by all fans, who felt Evans had improved the style of football and results, to some extent, during his time in charge.

SATURDAY 22nd DECEMBER 1906

Swindon were beaten 2-1 at Northampton Town in a Southern League fixture – and have not lost on this day since, in a run of 13 games without defeat.

TUESDAY 23rd DECEMBER 1986

Swindon made Fraser Digby's move from Manchester United permanent, paying what proved to be a bargain £32,500 for the keeper. He went on to play more games between the sticks than any other man in club history.

SATURDAY 24TH DECEMBER 1932

Swindon scored a fine pre-Christmas win over Cardiff City, beating the Bluebirds 6-2 in their Division Three (South) fixture, with outside-right Eddie Munnings getting his only hat-trick in a Swindon shirt. Syd Brookes, Ted Dransfield and Ted Braithwaite scored the other goals.

THURSDAY 25TH DECEMBER 1924

Jack Johnson and Cyril Daniel scored in a 2-1 win over Reading that kept Swindon's perfect home record in Division Three (South) intact. It's a tenth win out of ten. With three wins out of three at the end of the season before, it meant Town hadn't dropped a point at home in a club-record 13 matches – the last time they hadn't won was back at the start of April.

FRIDAY 25TH DECEMBER 1936

The traditional Christmas Day morning kick off was a local derby, with Swindon away at Reading this time. Jimmy Cookson scored twice in a 2-2 draw before the players head back for their afternoon Christmas dinner. Twenty-four hours later they were back in action with another away game at Northampton Town.

THURSDAY 25TH DECEMBER 1958

Swindon played their last-ever Christmas Day fixture and they returned from west London with a point after a 2-2 draw at Brentford in Division Three. Bob Edwards scored twice.

FRIDAY 26TH DECEMBER 1930

Twenty-four hours after beating Fulham 4-1 at the County Ground, the Londoners exacted quick revenge by winning 6-1 at Craven Cottage. Even the Swindon goal was given to them by defender Sonny Gibbon. The result couldn't be explained by radical changes, as both sides fielded the same 11 players in both fixtures.

MONDAY 26TH DECEMBER 1938

Swindon record their biggest Boxing Day win to date, beating Newport County 8-0 in Division Three (South). Ben Morton's hat-trick spearheaded the win, while a Welshman, Cliff Francis, weighed in with two goals.

FRIDAY 26TH DECEMBER 2008

Swindon confirmed the appointment of ex-Bristol City boss Danny Wilson as their manager to replace Maurice Malpas shortly after he left Hartlepool United. It's thought that Colin Calderwood ended up being his closest rival for the job, with ex-Walsall boss Richard Money among the contenders during a prolonged search. Wilson though, wasn't able to make the game with Leyton Orient at Brisbane Road. However, Lee Peacock scored within 60 seconds to mark his old boss taking over, while Jack Smith netted a penalty as Swindon held on for a 2-1 win in an entertaining contest with Dave Byrne in caretaker charge for the final time.

TUESDAY 27TH DECEMBER 1938

Swindon's return match at Newport County, 24 hours after the 8-0 win, was almost as memorable as the original fixture. This time the Welsh side came out on top, winning 6-4. Future Swindon keeper Alex Ferguson was in goal for County in both matches.

SATURDAY 28TH DECEMBER 1901

Swindon lost 10-1 in an infamous Southern League defeat at Kettering Town, after goalkeeper Bob Menham missed the train to Northamptonshire and full-back Paddy Fagan was forced to play in goal.

SATURDAY 28TH DECEMBER 1985

Swindon hit the top of Division Four for the first time this season, having gone on a rip-roaring run of form after their poor start. Striker Colin Gordon got the only goal, a second-half winner, as Lou Macari's side ground out a 1-0 victory at Torquay United – the old club of keeper Kenny Allen. The victory at Plainmoor made it 24 points from the past 27, with eight wins out of a possible nine.

SATURDAY 29TH DECEMBER 1979

Swindon tried to keep the pressure on the sides at the top of Division Three, while juggling their priorities with a League Cup run. They came away from Brentford with a 3-1 win. Swindon were a goal down but led by half-time, with goals from Chris Kamara, Andy Rowland and Alan Mayes sealing victory.

WEDNESDAY 29TH DECEMBER 1993

Swindon fans descended on Hillsborough in huge numbers for their Premier League fixture and they saw a thrilling game, with Swindon leading 2-1 after 20 minutes as Craig Maskell took advantage of a rare start to score. Sheffield Wednesday's equaliser was a controversial one, as referee Philip Don allowed play to continue with keeper Fraser Digby prostrate inside the penalty area with a dislocated shoulder. Gordon Watson took advantage to score as the Town defence just couldn't clear the ball. Watson then beat sub keeper Nicky Hammond almost immediately, but Craig Maskell's late bullet header earned a deserved point.

SATURDAY 29TH DECEMBER 2001

Andy King got his first win since returning as manager as Swindon made a fast start against Bury to win 3-1. Bobby Howe and Andy Gurney scored twice in the opening minutes, and after John Newby scored, the on-loan Wayne Carlisle popped up with his second and final goal for the club to get three important points against a struggling side.

FRIDAY 30TH DECEMBER 1994

Swindon completed a permanent move for defender Ian Culverhouse, paying Norwich what looks like a bargain £250,000. The defender sadly misses the last two months of the season, a big loss as the club battle against a second successive relegation while also looking for a place in the League Cup Final. The deal was funded by the sale of striker Keith Scott.

THURSDAY 31ST DECEMBER 1981

Swindon took a gamble on a gangly striker from non-league Oswestry Town, when they pay £10,000 for forward Jimmy Quinn. It proved to be a shrewd investment by John Trollope, as Quinn repaid the fee many times over with both his goals, and his sale.

SATURDAY 31ST DECEMBER 1983

Jimmy Quinn celebrated his two years at the club by scoring Swindon's equaliser in a 1-1 Division Four draw with Peterborough United at London Road. Quinn beats a promising goalkeeper called David Seaman after being preferred to Alan Mayes in the starting line-up.